WHEN
THERE
ARE NO EASY
ANSWERS

WHEN THERE ARE NO EASY ANSWERS

*Thinking Differently About
God, Suffering, and Evil*

JOHN S. FEINBERG

Kregel
Publications

Dedicated to Josiah Stephen, Jonathan Seth,
and Jeremy Samuel.
Three gifts of God's love.

CONTENTS

PREFACE

There are many hurting people in our world today. No one can predict where and when tragedy may strike. Sometimes because we haven't faced serious affliction, we think it won't happen to us. Especially if we live our lives in conformity to God's Word, we assume that we won't have to face the most horrible kinds of tragedies. Christians know the story of Job, but everyone agrees that his was a special case. It is natural to assume that most who suffer terribly do so in punishment for some serious sin.

All of these common conceptions seemed worthless when my family learned something far beyond our worst fears. This book recounts what happened and what I have learned from it. This is not a book that I ever imagined I would write. And of course, I wish I hadn't learned the things I'll share in the way I did. But God's will and way don't always match what we would like to happen. Hence, I have a story that I never would have imagined. I share it because I hope it will help you if you are suffering, and I also trust that it will help those who minister to the afflicted.

This book has been in print before. Though it was tempting not to republish it, I have found that when I tell our story, people who hear it find it quite helpful. Often they ask if our story is in print, because they can think of family members or friends with whom they would like to share it. And so I pursued republication. It has also been a long time since the previous edition was in print, and various things have happened since the book was last published. The major themes of the earlier editions have not changed, but I have amplified some of them, and have added information about what we are currently experiencing as we continue to deal with my wife's disease.

Since this book is about struggles with suffering and evil, some readers may wonder why I haven't referred to other classical treatments of the topic. C. S. Lewis's *A Grief Observed*, D. A. Carson's *How Long, O Lord?*, and Nicholas Wolterstorff's *Lament for a Son* are all very well worth reading. I don't refer to them only because this book is not the result of an academic research project. It is, instead, the story of my family, and what has happened to us is in various ways unique. The story is a very personal one—one that I would just as soon have kept private. However, through the leading of the Lord and the encouragement of others, I realized many years ago that I should write this book, but I wanted it to be *our* story told in *my* own way and words. I offer it as a personal testimony of God's specific dealings with me and my family.

To produce any book requires the encouragement and help of various people. I must initially express my appreciation to Dennis Hillman and Kregel Publications. Their willingness to reprint this book is most appreciated! A special word of thanks is due to Dawn Anderson, editor at Kregel, for her tireless efforts. I am confident that none of us view this book as a money-making venture but rather as an opportunity to minister to hurting people.

There are, of course, other books about suffering, but often Christian discussions of personal struggles with suffering tend to minimize the severity of afflictions, and in some cases even attempt to convince readers that the evils confronted are not actually evil after all. All of that may make sense to people who have never had to deal with anything genuinely tragic, but real people dealing with horrible situations know different. You should not expect anyone to be comforted—and you cannot comfort anyone—if your basic strategy is to try to convince them that what has happened is not really so bad after all, and that the appropriate response from a Christian is to rejoice over what is happening. Don't expect to find such platitudes in the pages of this book! Terrible things do happen to godly people. Don't think that the way to help them deal with the evil that has happened is to minimize the cause of their pain. Even though Jesus knew that he would resurrect a dead Lazarus, when he saw Lazarus's dead body and saw the grief of Martha and Mary (Lazarus's sisters), he wept (John 11:35)! We are not required to be happy that evil has happened to anyone.

Many years ago, in preparation for an earlier edition of this book, Pat wrote an afterword, and I am including it in this edition. It reflects accurately the way she has always handled this disease. I believe you will find it to be moving and encouraging as you confront your own trials and afflictions.

If you are suffering at this time, I hope this book will minister to you. Some points I make in the book may bear rereading at a later time when you have had more time to deal with the trials you are facing. The things that have been and are helpful to me didn't happen all at the same time, so I fully understand that you may find parts of this book helpful at one time and others helpful at another. I also hope and pray that this book will be of use to those who minister to the afflicted. May God be pleased to use it in these ways to his glory!

PRELUDE
TO A PROBLEM

November 4, 1987, was the day that changed my life forever. Let me back up. I grew up in a Christian home, though not an ordinary one. My father and mother were born into extremely devout Orthodox Jewish homes. My mom was born in Kovel, Ukraine, just a few years before World War I began, while my dad was born and raised in Pittsburgh, Pennsylvania. What are the chances, humanly speaking, that the two of them would ever meet? Of course, chance had nothing to do with it. Mom was one of those immigrants you sometimes read about who came to America, first entering at Ellis Island in New York harbor. Her father had gone to the United States seven years before the rest of the family came. Eventually, the family reunited and settled on the south side of Chicago.

During Dad's college days at the University of Pittsburgh, the Lord revealed himself to Dad, and by the end of 1929 he accepted Jesus as his Messiah and Savior. In her teenage years, Mom was given the gospel by missionaries to the Jews, and she too received Jesus as her Messiah and Savior.

Of course, both of their families were horrified. Neither Mom nor Dad wanted to hurt their families, but what could they do? The truth that Jesus is Israel's long-awaited Messiah could not be denied. Eventually, Mom wanted to go for Bible training at Moody Bible Institute. Her parents insisted that she give up her new religion or move out of the family home. Mom loved her family, but, determined to follow her Lord, Mom enrolled at Moody and moved into the dorms.

Not long after accepting Christ, Dad was gripped by a clear call to full-time ministry. Following that call, he enrolled in Dallas Seminary. In a brief five-year span, he earned a Bachelor of Divinity, a Master of Theology, and a Doctor of Theology degrees. During those student years, Dad was already in demand as a Bible teacher and preacher. On one occasion, he had a speaking engagement in Michigan, representing Chosen People Ministries (the mission that led him to the Lord). Those were the days before regular and reliable travel by air, so the options were to go either by train or by car. Dad and a friend went by car, and their route led them through Chicago where they stopped for the night. Dad's traveling companion had a friend at Moody. The Moody student told Dad and his friend that there was a social event scheduled for Moody students the next day, and invited them to attend.

At that social, Dad met Mom, and before too long, they were engaged. The plan was for Mom to finish at Moody and stay in Chicago while Dad finished doctoral studies at Dallas. On May 14, 1935, Dad graduated from Dallas Seminary, and the same day, in the home of Dr. and Mrs. Lewis Sperry Chafer, Mom and Dad were married.

Dad was already teaching at Dallas Seminary even before he finished his degree programs. He stayed on faculty until 1948 when he accepted a call to go to Southern California, teach at the Bible Institute of Los Angeles, and eventually start Talbot Theological

Seminary. During Mom and Dad's years in Dallas, my brother, sister, and I were born. I was two years old when the family moved to California.

As a child, I often heard about how Jews throughout history had been persecuted for no other reason than that they were Jews. I learned slowly but surely that there is a lot of pain and suffering in this life, even for those who trust Christ as their Savior. And I had a vivid illustration of that truth in my own family. During her childhood, my mom had not gotten proper nutrition—Jewish peasants living in Ukraine could hardly make ends meet. As a result of this and other physical difficulties, throughout her adult years Mom was forced to deal with one physical problem after another. In fact, I cannot remember a day in my life while my mother was alive that she was not in pain and dealing with one health concern or another. So I grew up fully aware that no one gets exemption from suffering just because he or she accepts Christ and obeys the commands of Scripture.

I was also taught by my parents and in church that the key in life is to find God's will and obey it. Christian hymns like "Have Thine Own Way, Lord" and "Where He Leads Me I Will Follow" express those desires quite well. But I wondered whether it is actually possible to know God's will for our lives. I think most Christians have the same desires and questions.

As I grew up, I sought God's will about what he wanted me to do with my life, and about whom I should marry. By the time I was twenty-six, I was certain that I had found God's answers to both questions. And I have never doubted the answers.

But after November 4, 1987, I began to have questions that I'd never before thought to ask. Questions like, does God ever hide information from us in order to get us to do his will? Is it possible to seek God's will, find it, and do it, and then discover that what God wanted brought great suffering and evil into your life? If that happened, wouldn't it mean that God had tricked or even deceived you into doing his will?

After your initial shock from reading that paragraph, you are probably thinking, "That's just crazy! That couldn't happen, because God just doesn't work that way. Scripture tells us to ask God to show us his will. In fact, Jesus instructed his disciples to ask God to do his will on earth as it is done in heaven (Matt. 6:10). So, of course, God's people should ask him to do his will in their own lives. In fact, the apostle John offers the following encouragement: 'This is the confidence which we have before Him, that, if we ask anything according to His will, He hears us. And if we know that He hears us in whatever we ask, we know that we have the requests which we have asked from Him'" (1 John 5:14–15 NASB).

That seems rather clear. We must seek God's will and as long as we pray in accordance with it, he will grant our requests. But if we pray according to God's will, he wouldn't give us something evil, would he? After all, remember what Jesus said:

> Or what man is there among you who, when his son asks for a loaf, will give him a stone? Or if he asks for a fish, he will not give him a snake, will he? If you then, being evil, know how to give good gifts to your children, how much more will your Father who is in heaven give what is good to those who ask Him! (Matt. 7:9–11 NASB)

Surely, then, if God reveals his will and we do it, evil won't befall us. God won't give us a stone when we ask for a loaf or a snake when we ask for a fish, especially not when we ask according to his will for us. Thoughts to the contrary must be absurd, if not blasphemous. They imagine the unthinkable, the impossible.

Or do they? For most of my life I would not have even thought to raise such questions. Oh, I knew bad things happen to good people, and for much of my life I wondered why God lets that happen to those he loves so dearly. As I grew up I was fascinated by the story of Job, especially with what we learn in Job 1–2 about how it all began. Being Jewish by background I heard my parents speak frequently about the Holocaust, and I was horrified at such inhumanity to man. Even more, I couldn't understand how a loving God would allow this to happen to his "chosen people." And then there was my mother and her many physical ailments. She was seldom so ill for days on end that she couldn't run the household, but I could tell that she constantly functioned while dealing with a great amount of pain.

That's not the whole story about my mother, however. Her life had been filled with persecution. She was born in a little Ukrainian village in the early twentieth century. Peasants at that time didn't matter to the government, and Jewish peasants were worth even less. Not long after her birth, the Bolshevik Revolution came to Russia. In the midst of the persecution, she and her family eventually fled from their homeland and came to America. But experiencing cruelty at the hands of soldiers and hiding to avoid capture left indelible marks on her personality. For many years into adulthood, she had nightmares about her childhood.

All of this made me wonder why a God of love would allow such suffering and hardship to happen to innocent people. At various times in my life I pondered whether I would still want to worship and serve God if he rewarded my faithfulness with severe affliction. But I didn't expect to personally address such questions, because I never dreamed that terrible affliction might come in the process of seeking, finding, and doing God's will. Nor would I have thought that God's ways might include getting someone to do his will by withholding information—information which, if known, would have kept them from doing what God wanted, but also would have avoided much personal pain and anguish. That would seem to be trickery, even deceit, and it would also be cruel, especially if by doing God's will we ended up in the midst of severe affliction. Who would think God does this to get his way?

And yet, in the late 1980s something happened that led me to ask such questions and to think the unthinkable. For reasons mentioned above, throughout my life I have thought a lot about the problem of evil, the question of why there is evil and suffering in our world if there is a God who loves us enough to stop it and has the power to do so. In fact, I even wrote my doctoral dissertation in philosophy on the problem of evil. I had learned that there is a difference between asking why there is evil *in general* if an all-loving, all-powerful God exists, and asking why God allows a *specific* evil to happen to someone.

Philosophers and theologians debate intelletually how the evil in our world is consistent with an all-powerful, all-loving God. On the other hand, the *personal experience of* evil creates a different kind of problem. Those dealing with personal affliction may find that their suffering disrupts their relationship with God. They may find it hard to serve or even worship God. They may even be tempted to stop believing in God altogether. The personal experience of evil precipitates a crisis of faith in the believer's life. As one philosopher wisely observes, "Such a problem calls, not for philosophical enlightenment, but for pastoral care."*

I read that statement many years ago. Intellectually, I agreed with it, but experientially, I didn't really understand it. I had always seen the problem of evil as a major hindrance to getting non-Christians to consider Christ. I knew it could be devastating to the faith of Christians as well. But I thought that as long as one had intellectual answers to explain why God allowed evil in the world, that would satisfy those who suffer. I thought those answers would give the necessary strength to withstand the afflictions. Even more, I believed that if comforters could just point to all the positive things God might use affliction to accomplish in the lives of those who suffer, the afflicted might reach a point where they could even thank God for the affliction.

When I saw others struggle in their relationship with God because of some tragedy, I naïvely thought that if I could just

---

*Alvin Plantinga, *God, Freedom, and Evil* (New York: Harper and Row, 1974), 63–64.

talk with them and offer some intellectual answers, that would resolve everything. I was somewhat impatient with them when they seemed unable to move past their struggles. In principle, I agreed that sufferers need pastoral care, but I thought that a lot of that care involved explaining intellectually God's purposes in allowing evil. Maybe personal struggles in the face of evil aren't problems needing philosophical enlightenment, but a healthy dose of academic philosophy couldn't hurt. Or so I thought.

Since November 4, 1987, I have come to see things quite differently, especially because of the way evil has deeply touched my wife and family. Before this happened, I couldn't have written this book. I thought it was enough just to have intellectual answers, and that those answers would be sufficient for handling any personal evil that might come into my life. For a long time after we learned about my wife's condition, I found it too painful to speak about what had happened, let alone write about it.

What happened that so revolutionized my thinking? Let me share my story. Like many people, I grew up, went to school, got married, and began a career in relatively trouble-free circumstances. There were problems and afflictions along the way, like most people experience, but nothing catastrophic or truly tragic. I knew that those who stand for Christ can expect to suffer, and I had a vivid illustration of that in my mother's constant faith despite illness after illness. I remembered as well that in the early 1950s my father almost died, but God marvelously preserved his life. Dad had undergone an operation at the University of California, Los Angeles Medical Center, and recovery at home was going quite smoothly. But one evening after I had gone to bed, he began to hemorrhage. No matter what Mom tried, the flow of blood continued. She took him to several local hospitals but was advised that she had to take him to see the doctor who had done the operation. Unfortunately, the UCLA Medical Center and Dad's doctor were some thirty-five to forty miles away. And that was in the days before the elaborate freeway system in Los Angeles had been built. The situation seemed hopeless, but Mom wouldn't give up. She and my sister got Dad into the car and set out for UCLA. By the time they arrived Dad had lost a substantial amount of blood. The doctors said his blood level was so low that he should have been dead. Thankfully, he wasn't, and they were able to stabilize his condition. Dad recovered, but my realization that I could have lost my father indelibly showed me how tenuous a hold on life any of us has.

Because of these experiences, I figured that there were more troubles coming. I assumed that they would be like the rest I had endured—annoying, frustrating, and painful to a certain degree, but nothing totally devastating. After all, I reasoned, once one goes a certain distance with Christ and reaches a certain level of spiritual maturity, even really big problems won't derail spiritual growth. There might be temporary setbacks in one's relationship with the Lord, but they would soon be over. Surely my dad's near brush with death and my mom's continued faith in spite of constantly dealing with painful physical problems confirmed such thoughts.

All of that changed for me on November 4, 1987, when I learned something that went far beyond my worst nightmare. For some years my wife, Pat, had experienced certain physical difficulties. As best as we can figure, there were signs of problems as early as 1979. At first there was a periodic twitching of her shoulder. And, as each day wore on, Pat became extremely tired. These symptoms weren't painful, and neither Pat nor I thought of them as real physical problems. She thought that her shoulder moving was just a habit she could break. I thought her lack of energy wasn't unusual for a woman with two small children under the age of five. As the years passed, the difficulties became more pronounced, and were now in other parts of her body as well. It seemed that the movements came once every few minutes. One evening, without telling Pat, I decided to time how frequently she moved. To my surprise and dismay she had these movements every few seconds. This could no longer be interpreted as a habit that she could break.

We decided that we had to find out what the problem was and get it corrected. Pat eventually went to a neurologist who made the diagnosis. When she came home from the doctor's office, I could tell something was wrong, but I never could have imagined what she was about to tell me. The doctor had diagnosed her as having Huntington's chorea.

At the time, I knew nothing about Huntington's disease. I was forced to learn very quickly. Huntington's is a genetically transmitted disease that involves the premature deterioration of cells deep within the brain. Brain cells are killed, and the result isn't entirely unlike what happens when an older person shows signs of dementia as a result of aging. Symptoms are both physical and psychological.

On the physical side, there is gradual loss of control of voluntary bodily movement. At first Pat had problems with her balance, and found it increasingly difficult to walk more than a short distance. Eventually, she was not able to stand or walk at all, even with help. As of this writing, she has for many years been confined to a wheelchair, and must be lifted to get in and out of it. The physical deterioration also resulted in slurred speech, and gradually she also lost her ability to swallow. In 2001 a feeding tube was inserted into her stomach, and for the last decade or so she has been able to get food and fluid only through that tube.

On the mental and psychological side of this disease, initially she began to be forgetful. Gradually, she lost her ability to pay attention to anything for very long. It has now been more than five and a half years since she has spoken a word. If I can get her to look me straight in the eyes and if I speak slowly and don't try to discuss complicated ideas, I can see from a slight reaction in her eyes that she understands what I am saying. But I have no idea whether even a few moments later she remembers what was said to her. And she cannot respond verbally to what she hears. Because she can't talk, I don't know what she thinks about most of the time.

Then, as with many Huntington's patients, depression is a major problem, though Pat has taken medication for it and has to this point responded well to the medication. Huntington's patients can also have hallucinations and can ultimately become paranoid schizophrenic. Thankfully, so far we have not seen evidence of these symptoms, but one of the frustrating aspects of this disease is that you never know how rapidly it will progress or which symptoms anyone with it will exhibit. In fact, it is impossible to make any generalizations about the course of the disease, even if one uses the patient's own condition as the basis for predicting future symptoms. Some potential symptoms may never show themselves, while others that seemed initially transitory may never go away.

Though someone might begin to deal with Huntington's as a teenager, symptoms usually begin in one's thirties or forties. It is a slow-developing disease, but over several decades it takes its toll, and it is fatal. Medications may minimize symptoms, but there is still no known cure. Doctors had only identified the chromosome involved just a few years prior to my wife's diagnosis. It wasn't until 1993 that the exact genetic marker was discovered. Around the turn of the century, researchers discovered how this disease kills brain cells. They just haven't yet figured out how to stop it from happening.

Though all of this is very bad news, the situation is actually even worse. Huntington's disease is controlled by a dominant gene. This means that only one parent needs to have it in order to transfer it to their children. Each child has a fifty-fifty chance of getting it, but as mentioned, symptoms don't usually start to appear before one's thirties or forties. Our three sons were born prior to Pat's diagnosis.

Since Huntington's is controlled by a dominant gene, those who have the gene get the disease. If they don't get the disease, they can't be a carrier. There are tests to determine beforehand how likely it is that one will have it. The accuracy of those tests increased as researchers zeroed in on and finally discovered the exact gene involved. Still, there is a real dilemma about taking the test versus remaining in the dark about one's chances of getting the disease.

During an office visit many years ago, I asked Pat's doctor what was involved in getting tested so that I could find out what percentage of the cost the health insurance company would cover. The doctor replied that whatever we did, we should avoid reporting any of it to the insurance company. If the test showed that one of our sons would get the disease, it might be impossible for him to get health insurance. In addition, prospective employers might refuse to hire someone known to have the gene for Huntington's. During the 1990s laws were passed by the US Congress to make this sort of discrimination illegal. But anyone should know that despite whatever the law says, there are usually "creative" ways of getting around it. On the other hand, if our sons didn't take the test, they would have to make important life decisions—about career, marriage, and having children—in the dark.

When news of Pat's disease came, my initial reactions were shock, confusion, and disbelief. How could this be happening? Before we were married, we knew that Pat's mother had mental problems. At the time of our wedding, she had been in a mental institution for five years. We asked several people how likely it was that this might happen to Pat, believing all along that it was purely psychological. Psychologists assured us that if Pat were to have such problems, they would have already surfaced. Since she was in her twenties and nothing of that sort had happened, we were led to believe there was no need to worry. We never imagined that there was a physiological base to my mother-in-law's condition or that the difficulty could be passed genetically to my wife. Nor, apparently, did anyone else in her family. Immediate family members knew nothing about this, and others who might have known said nothing. My father-in-law had at one time heard the name of the disease, but didn't ask for details about it. Everyone who might have known the truth either didn't know it or withheld the information. Before we started our family, we checked again to see if anything hereditary could be passed on to harm the children. Again, we were assured there was nothing to fear.

We had wanted to discover whether it was God's will for us to marry and later to have children. We told God that we were willing to do whatever he wanted. If he didn't want us to marry, we asked him to show us that. One way to do so would be for us to learn that Pat could get her mother's disease. We searched for this information, but we didn't find it. When we didn't find such information, in addition to other factors I'll mention later, we were led to believe that God wanted us to marry.

So when Pat was diagnosed with Huntington's, we found it hard to believe that this was happening, but it was, anyway. Professionals who were supposed to know about such things had said it wouldn't, but it did. It was also unbelievable because of the basis of the doctor's diagnosis. He did nothing more than watch Pat move and ask her about her family history. No genetic tests or tests of any other kind were done that day. I complained that this was all too inferential. Such skimpy data shouldn't warrant that conclusion. No philosopher would accept that kind of argument.

For several months I was torn between the hope that it wasn't true and the fear that Pat's problems could be nothing else. When a second opinion by a specialist doing research on the disease confirmed the diagnosis, all hope that she didn't have Huntington's collapsed.

HOW DISMAL
LIFE CAN SEEM

After my wife's initial diagnosis, I was besieged by a host of emotions and reactions. Even to this day, I still wrestle at times with some of those feelings. I believe others who experience tragedy undergo similar reactions. If we are to minister to those who are hurting, we must understand how they feel.

Denial

In chapter 1 I alluded to one of my first reactions—denial. When Pat first told me the diagnosis, I asked on what basis the doctor made this assessment. Pat answered that he watched her move and asked about her family history. I asked if he did any tests or thought any should be done. There were no tests and no plans for any tests. I thought it was absolutely absurd to offer such a horrible diagnosis on such flimsy evidence. Of course, at the time I knew only what Pat told me about Huntington's. Most diseases I could think of had to be confirmed by a test or series of tests, so I thought the same must be true for this disease. Since Huntington's is caused by a defective gene, I couldn't believe there could be any certainty that Pat had it without doing a genetic test. To this day she has never had such a test, so certainly at the beginning I thought it impossible to find this diagnosis believable, based as it was on so little evidence. I thought it was good that I am a philosopher, because as one, I could detect faulty reasoning, and this was, I believed, a clear example of an inference unwarranted by the evidence.

But no amount of logic, philosophy, or any other sort of reasoning could *prove* that the doctor was wrong. And so I had two reactions at once: belief that the doctor didn't know what he was talking about and fear that he was probably right anyway. In the days and weeks that followed that first diagnosis, I did everything I could think of to disprove this "theory" about what was happening to Pat. Whenever someone mentioned a disease, I asked about the symptoms, and if they seemed even vaguely like what Pat was experiencing, I imagined that her real problem was this other disease. But whenever I asked a physician whether she might really have this or that illness, the physician always had an explanation of why that couldn't be so. As we sought opinions from other doctors, I became more discouraged as they refuted theory after theory.

As we came closer to a final confirmation of the original diagnosis, I was still holding out hope that it wasn't so, but began to process what it would mean if the doctors were right. I can emphatically say that such an emotional state is no fun whatsoever. You are pulled in one direction by the defiant denial that this isn't really what's happening, and at the same time you are dragged in another direction by the realization of all the horrible implications if the doctors are right. Torn between defiance and despair, you feel as if you have just endured a boxing match with the heavyweight champion of the world who, round after round, has relentlessly pummeled your head and body.

Denial isn't unusual when tragedy first strikes. In my case, it lasted several months but came to a crushing end when we saw a doctor who was doing research on Huntington's. I had gotten Pat's mother's chart from the hospital in New York where she spent the last decade of her life. I brought it to the specialist. He looked at it, observed Pat's symptoms, and confirmed that she had Huntington's. I raised one of my alternate theories, and he turned to a page of the chart, pointed to several notes, and said emphatically, "That's Huntington's." He also ordered a brain scan to confirm the diagnosis. The scan showed little deterioration, but the fact that it showed any was evidence enough. By that point, however, I had already given up the fight—there simply were no adequate grounds to deny what had become painfully clear to all of us.

Hopelessness and Helplessness

While I was hanging on to hope that the doctors were wrong but fearing the worst, and after confirmation that the diagnosis was correct, the predominant reactions I experienced were feelings of hopelessness and helplessness. There had been problems before, but usually there was some way out. In fact, I could usually figure out something to do. But not this time. Huntington's is a disease with no known cure.

The situation seemed absolutely hopeless. I would have to watch my wife, whom I dearly love, slowly deteriorate and die. As the disease progressed, maybe she wouldn't even know me. Even worse, maybe she would know me, but would turn against me as she imagined that I had turned against her. After all, my mother-in-law had misjudged my father-in-law's reasons for putting her in a mental institution for the last years of her life. Irrational fears and feelings are the norm, not the exception, with this disease. Eventually Pat as I knew her would be gone, and yet it still wouldn't be over. The same thing could happen to each of our sons. I remember thinking that this threat of doom would hang over our family every day for the rest of our lives. There was no morally acceptable way to escape this situation. There was only one person who could do anything about this, and it appeared at that time that God wasn't going to help. Beyond this, it seemed that he had led us into this situation rather than keeping us from it. As I grieved over the hopelessness of our situation, I realized how dismal life can seem.

Beyond the hopelessness, I felt helpless to do a thing. I was experiencing physical problems myself that were only aggravated by the stress from this news. Before long I came to a point where I was barely able to do my work. I wasn't much help to my family either. I wanted at least to comfort Pat and help her deal with this distressing news, but all along she has handled this situation far better than I. Maybe she was struggling with what was happening, but she wouldn't say so. She saw how devastating the news was to me and probably thought that if she complained about what was happening, it might only make me feel worse. So she said little about it and went on with her daily routine of caring for the family. She didn't seem to need comfort from me or anyone else. When someone would ask her how she was doing, she never complained. Instead, she would ask them to pray for me and our kids. I felt locked out of her life and unable to be of any help at this most critical time in our family's life. Whatever therapeutic value there might have been for me in comforting her was lost.

Our children's reactions weren't much different. Before we told them what was happening, they knew something was wrong. I told Pat that we shouldn't trouble them with this news until we knew for certain that the diagnosis was correct. Once it was confirmed, we sat down with them and shared the news. In the conversation, I told them that other people would probably say things about this disease that were wrong. Instead of listening to others, they should talk with us about it. If they had questions we couldn't answer, we would get the answers for them. Each understood some of what was happening, but all understood that their mom was very sick. Over the years of their childhood, they were hesitant to talk about the disease. When we would ask them how they were doing, they would say that they were doing fine and that they really didn't think about this disease much at all. Again, I could not offer them comfort as they seemed not to be bothered by what might happen to them. Only as they became adults did they share their true feelings. They are deeply saddened by what is happening to their mother, and the chance that they may get this disease makes it impossible to think about the future without fear, grief, and uncertainty. But when we first broke the news to them (and for a long time after that), they didn't seem to need or want comfort and encouragement about their situation.

Though your troubles and trials are probably different from mine, I suspect you have had similar feelings of hopelessness and helplessness if you have had to deal with some major tragedy. Along with those feelings also comes a sense of abandonment. At such times, you feel that there is no answer and no help. Yes, there are friends and family, but what can they do? They aren't miracle-workers. In our case, even the doctors couldn't cure this disease, so what could others do?

Abandonment

Something else heightens the feeling of abandonment. Invariably when news like this comes, people are very concerned; but for various reasons, they tend to stay away. Some may fear that they will say the wrong thing and only make matters worse. They just stay away rather than taking the chance of sticking their foot in their mouth. Others may think that unless they have something "brilliant" to say that will remove all the pain and heartache, they should avoid the sufferer. Believing that they have nothing special to say, they don't communicate at all with the sufferer. And perhaps some fear that if they went to the afflicted person, the sufferer might break down and cry over what has happened. Not knowing how to deal with that if it should occur, the friend chooses to keep his or her distance.

However, remaining at a distance only confirms the worst fears of the sufferer. There is already the feeling of abandonment; the afflicted feels as though he or she has been given an enormous burden to bear for the rest of his or her life, and there will be no one to help. When family and friends keep their distance, they communicate that this is likely true. As time goes by, the shock of the awful news subsides, and people seem to forget about what is happening. Increasingly, they ask less and less about how the family is doing.

The deeper fear is not just that family and friends have abandoned you, but that God is no longer there. It doesn't matter how much you have sensed God's presence before, at times like this he seems absent. And when you know that God is the only one who can do anything about the problem, it is especially painful to sense his departure. You can't help but feel that you are facing a totally hopeless situation, and that you are facing it all alone!

Anger and Confusion

These feelings of abandonment are also accompanied by anger. The anger may not be particularly rational, but it is very real. I was angry that this was happening to us. I never expected exemption from problems just because I am a Christian, but I never thought something like this would happen. In one fell stroke, we learned that my whole family, including potential future generations, was under a dark cloud of doom. That kind of catastrophe wasn't supposed to happen.

I was angry at family members who knew and didn't tell us. I was angry at the doctors who knew and never explained it to the family. And I was angry at family members who didn't know even though they could have asked the doctors for an explanation.

Honestly, if I had known that it was even possible for Pat to get Huntington's disease, I probably wouldn't have married her. Pat has said that had she known of this possibility, she probably wouldn't have married at all. If we had learned of her condition before starting a family, we wouldn't have had children. Any ethicist would say that it is morally dubious to subject someone to this fate if you know this could happen! In short, with one diagnosis my wife and children were condemned to a life of anxiety, uncertainty, and possibly then a slow and painful death. If someone had told us the truth before we married, we could have avoided putting more lives in jeopardy, and could have had a much more normal life.

Though I didn't want to admit it, I was also angry at God. I knew that anger with God was foolish, because God hadn't done this. Nothing in or out of Scripture obligates God to keep things like this from happening. Beyond that, it was foolish to be angry with the only person who could do anything about this bleak situation. Anyway, who was I, the creature, to contest the Creator? As the apostle Paul says (Rom. 9:19–21), the creature has no right to haul the Creator into the courtroom of human moral judgments and put him on trial as though he has done something wrong. God has total power and authority over me. It is foolish to be angry with the One who has such total control over my every move.

Still, it is human nature to be angry and expect something different from God. There are questions about why we have to deal with this affliction when others don't. It's not that I would wish this disease on anyone else. Rather, the point is that others have escaped, so why shouldn't we as well? It just didn't seem fair that we have to bear this burden.

In my case, the complaint wasn't just that God had allowed this to happen to us. I felt that God had somehow misled me, even tricked me. When Pat and I first met, we were sure there was no way we would marry. I was preparing for a teaching ministry in the United States, and she was headed to the mission field in Africa. Pat graduated from Nyack College and then applied to a number of mission boards to pursue her calling. No doors opened. She decided to attend Wheaton grad school to do an MA in Christian education. Another degree on her résumé would likely make her more attractive to mission boards, and she could surely use her training on the mission field. We continued to date and our relationship grew, but I feared that we were in for disappointment if we continued, because God was leading us in different directions.

Before I met Pat I had been engaged to be married. In that case, I had clearly run ahead of the Lord. By God's grace I came to see that, and I broke off the engagement. But the experience emphasized how extremely careful I had to be in choosing a life partner. Above all, I had decided to seek and follow God's leading. It didn't pay to test God by continuing a relationship that seemed outside his will.

I sensed that I knew what Pat and I had to do. One night I went to see her, intending to end our relationship. I was sure God wouldn't want us to defy his will to send us in different directions. I shared this with Pat and she agreed, though neither of us wanted it to end. At one point, I suggested that I would tell Pat what led me to believe God wanted me in a teaching ministry, and she should tell me what had made her believe that God wanted her in Africa. As Pat and I talked, it was clear that she had a definite call to full-time ministry, but I heard nothing that indicated a clear call to foreign missions. We decided to pray independently about it, asking the Lord to end our relationship (as painful as that would be), if he didn't want us together. We would pray about this for a month and then make a decision. In the meantime we continued to see each other; we just agreed not to talk about our relationship until the month was over.

Rather than destroying the relationship, the Lord made it abundantly clear in various ways that he wanted us to marry. I'm sure many have heard stories of women who were called to the mission field, but fell in love with someone, married him, and never went into missions. As time passed, the marriage turned sour and in some instances ended in divorce. The woman realized that God had definitely wanted her on the mission field; she had missed God's best for her life, and now she had nothing.

As common as such stories are, Pat talked with people who had stories with just the opposite outcome. She heard of women who believed God wanted them on the mission field. Before going to the field, however, they met someone and fell in love. Rather than marrying, they left their homeland to serve God in missions, believing that such was God's will. However, God hadn't really called them to missions, and the mission experience was a disaster. Before long they had to give up and return home. In the meantime, however, their prospective husband had married someone else. God actually wanted these women to marry instead of go into missions, but they had misread God's direction for their life. Now they had nothing—no ministry and no husband.

So, Pat came to see that when given a choice between missions and marriage, choosing missions isn't always God's will. In addition, as Pat and I reflected on what was happening, we concluded that it was natural for her to think God wanted her in Africa. She had been very active in her home church and its youth group. Her minister of youth had been a missionary to Africa, and he constantly spoke of the need for missionaries to go there. In such circumstances, it would be very natural for a teenager to conclude that she should become a missionary to Africa. In fact, God often does use our life circumstances to call us to one vocation or another. But since there hadn't been any occasion when Pat had felt God's specific call to Africa, it seemed that the circumstances might be misleading her.

Through this whole process of talking to other Christians and reflecting on God's leading in her life (Pat was even able to talk with her former youth pastor about this because he and his family were living in Wheaton at the time), Pat became convinced that God wanted us to marry. And I was convinced too. As I grew up, I had often wondered if you could be sure that the person you planned to marry was the right one. I figured that at least on your wedding day, you could be pretty sure you were marrying the right person, but not absolutely certain. That could only come after being married for a while and then seeing that you had chosen correctly. However, in light of how God had so clearly led us, I knew beyond a shadow of a doubt that God wanted me to marry Pat. Indeed, married life confirmed that.

I don't know whether most people, even if God does want them to marry, are certain on their wedding day that this is so. But I was absolutely certain, and I think God gave me that assurance in part because he knew that we would have to deal with Huntington's. With or without a clear sense of God's will that we marry, we would eventually get the diagnosis of Huntington's disease anyway. But without being certain that God wanted me to marry Pat, I might have assumed that the disease was God's way of informing me that I was wrong in thinking God wanted me to marry her. Who knows? Perhaps Pat and I might have even seen the disease as God's punishment for keeping her from the mission field. God precluded such thoughts by clearly showing us before we married that he definitely wanted us to marry. Having to deal with this disease is no reason for second-guessing whether God wanted us to marry one another.

But being so certain about the type of ministry God had for me and so certain that God wanted us to marry, perhaps you can better understand why I felt I had been deceived. The Lord knew the demands of the ministry to which he had called me. He also knew that I needed a wife to help me, and that if I were really to give myself to the work he was giving me, my wife should be at least relatively healthy. My dad had a very fruitful ministry of the sort I envisioned. My mom suffered with various physical problems, and I had seen the strain that had put on Dad. But Mom was never incapacitated to the point where she couldn't function in the home on a consistent basis. I reasoned that God knew all of that, so he would give me at least a relatively healthy wife. Of course, I assumed that the Lord would give me a certain kind of ministry. I couldn't see how I could have a wife with Pat's condition and carry on any kind of ministry, let alone one in teaching and pastoring. It didn't occur to me at the time that God's plan for my ministry might be a bit different from what I envisioned. What I was thinking about the future made sense, and surely, as supremely rational, God would know that and would have plans to bring about that future in our lives. Pat's diagnosis of Huntington's, then, made no sense to me, and it shouldn't have made sense to God either. But all of these terrible things were happening, and I was angry that none of it made any sense. Had I misread God's will about marriage and ministry? But I had been ministering with God's blessing for fifteen years when Pat's diagnosis came. And Pat had proved to be the perfect wife for me, and we had three wonderful sons! Should they have never been born? How could that possibly be so?

You can see that I was not just angry but I was also very confused. And the confusion stemmed from more than what I've already shared. Because Pat's mom had spent five years in a mental institution by the time Pat and I met, when Pat and I began to talk seriously about marriage, we thought it wise to consult some professionals to see whether Pat might get whatever it was that her mother had. We talked with several psychiatrists about whether Pat's personality could become like her mother's. They assured us that if Pat were to have mental problems, they would already have shown up. Since there was no sign of anything wrong with Pat, we were assured that there was nothing to worry about. We put such worries aside and proceeded with wedding plans. But in 1987, fifteen years into our marriage, I learned the horrible truth, and I felt I had been tricked. I had been led down a path, only to learn that I wasn't getting what I thought I was!

I remember thinking repeatedly at the time that none of this made any sense. God is the supremely rational being, and yet it seemed that he was actualizing a contradiction in my life. The news of my wife's illness seemed to contradict the Lord's leading in my life over the previous fifteen years. I didn't know what to do, and I didn't even know what to think. At one point, I thought about Abraham. God had given him Isaac, the child of promise, only to tell him to sacrifice Isaac on Mt. Moriah. That must have made no more sense to Abraham than my situation made to me. Even so, Abraham had believed. He even believed that if he sacrificed Isaac, God would resurrect him from the dead (Heb. 11:19).

What incredible faith! I should be more like Abraham. Surely his situation should comfort and encourage me. But it didn't. I remembered only too quickly that it made sense for Abraham to believe because God had made very specific promises about this son (Gen. 12:1–3; 15:4–6; 17:15–19). God had made no such promises to me about my wife and children. He had made it clear that Pat and I should marry, and even saw to it that information likely to have kept us from marrying and having children was hidden. But he never promised that there would be no catastrophic illness. There had never been any promises about how long or how healthy a life any of us would have. Certainly, God could perform a miracle (as Abraham expected in Isaac's case) and heal Pat, but there were no guarantees that he would. As instructive as the example of Abraham and Isaac is, I had no right to take comfort from it.

I was also confused for another reason. I was raised around people who suffered greatly. As I mentioned, my mother had one physical problem after another. I am sure that it was in part because of her experiences that I became interested at an early age in the problem of pain and suffering. As I grew up, I thought about that problem repeatedly. In seminary, I wrote my Master of Divinity thesis on Job. Later, my Master of Theology thesis was devoted to God's sovereign control of all things and how that relates to human freedom. Then my doctoral dissertation dealt with the problem of evil considered philosophically. If anyone had thought about this problem and was prepared to face real affliction, surely it was

I. Yet when the events I have recounted occurred, I found little comfort in any of this intense intellectual reflection.

The truth is, I couldn't make sense of what was happening. I had all those intellectual answers, but none of them made any difference in how I felt on the personal level. As a professor of theology, surely I should understand what God was doing in this situation. On the contrary, I began wondering if in fact I really understood anything at all about God. The emotional and psychological pain was unrelenting, and the physical results from the stress and mental pain were devastating.

The Religious Problem of Evil

Why hadn't all my years of study, reflection, and writing on the problem of evil helped at this moment of personal crisis? I was experiencing a faith crisis, and none of this information I had stored away seemed to matter in the least. As I reflected on this, I came to a very significant realization. All my study and all the intellectual answers were of little help because the religious problem of evil (the problem about one's personal struggle with pain and suffering and how that affects one's relationship with God) is not primarily an intellectual problem. Instead, it is fundamentally an emotional one! People wrestling with evil do not require an intellectual discourse on how to justify God's ways to his creation. Such answers address the more abstract theological and philosophical problems about why there should be any evil at all or evil in the amounts present in our world if there is a God. My problem, instead, was about how in the midst of affliction I could find comfort, and how I could find it in myself to live with this God who wasn't stopping the suffering.

This does not mean that no spiritual truths or intellectual answers can help the sufferer. It means that many of those answers won't help with this problem and that others that do won't help at all stages in the sufferer's experience. They must be used at times when the emotional pain has healed enough so that they can make a difference.

At this point, I understood experientially that the religious problem of evil requires pastoral care rather than philosophical discussion. I can illustrate the point by a simple example.

Think of a little girl who goes out to play on a playground. Sometime during her play, she falls and skins her knee. She runs, screaming in pain, to her mother for comfort. Now, her mother has some choices. She may tell her daughter that this has happened because she was running too fast and wasn't watching where she was going; she must be more careful the next time. The mother might even explain (if she knows them) the laws of physics and causation that were operating to make her child's knee scrape just the size and shape it is. The mother might even expound for a few moments on the lessons God is trying to teach her child from this experience.

If the mother then asks her daughter if she understands, don't be surprised if the little girl responds, "Yes, Mommy, but it still hurts!" All the explanation at that moment doesn't stop her pain. The child doesn't want a discourse; she wants and needs her mother's hugs and kisses. There will be time for the discourse later; now she needs comfort!

The same is true for each of us as we struggle with the religious problem of evil. When the affliction first comes, we don't want or need a lengthy discourse to appeal to our mind because this isn't primarily an intellectual matter. Even if you have something absolutely profound to say about the situation and you say it, don't be surprised if we are too hurt and confused to absorb it. We need someone to let us pour out our heart, not someone to give us a lecture, regardless of how brilliant and instructive it might be. And we need something to take away the pain, and a very big part of that pain is not knowing what these events mean about how God feels toward us. Or how we should feel toward him.

RECIPES FOR DISASTER, OR, HOW NOT TO HELP THE AFFLICTED

If the religious problem of evil (the problem about personal struggles with pain and suffering) isn't primarily about justifying God's ways to man but about how to live with the God who doesn't stop the suffering, how can we help others through these difficult times? I can only answer in terms of things that weren't helpful to me and things that did make a difference.

Invariably, people try to say or do something they hope will help. Sometimes it does, but often people can be extremely insensitive, and this only drives the sufferer into further despair. No one means to do this; no one is trying to make the burden worse. Most just want to help. But despite good intentions, these would-be comforters often wind up doing more harm than good.

Some years ago a relative of mine was on vacation. While away, she learned that her home had burned to the ground, trapping and killing her son who was unable to escape. Her pastor tried to be of help, but made some significant mistakes in handling the situation. For one thing, he made very little attempt to see her and allow her to talk out her feelings. The few times he did say something, he expressed concern over the loss of her house and possessions. You can imagine how hurt she was. The loss of one's home and possessions is not insignificant, but in one way or another, most of those objects can be replaced. The loss of a loved one is the greatest loss one can suffer, for how does one replace a son? That pastor completely missed the point of her grief. By his insensitivity, he missed the opportunity to minister to her in her time of crisis, and hindered rather than helped the healing process.

Let me suggest some statements that are inappropriate to say.

"You must have committed some sin."

Someone may say, "There must be some great sin you've committed; otherwise this wouldn't be happening to you." I am very thankful that no one said this to me or my family, though it is a common reaction of some people when they hear of severe affliction. This was the reaction of many of Job's so-called comforters. They didn't really know why Job suffered, but they were sure it wouldn't look good for God if a righteous man suffered. Therefore, they reasoned that God would only allow this to happen to the guilty.

While it is true that God punishes sin, and that the wicked will have a day of judgment, Scripture is very clear that sometimes the ungodly do prosper (Ps. 73), while the righteous suffer (Job 1:8; 2:3; 1 Peter 4:12–19). The truth is that in most instances we don't really know whether someone suffers as a redeemed person or as a result of personal sin. Outwardly moral people may be great sinners, and even those who seem righteous may be guilty of some hidden sin. The story of the rich man and Lazarus (Luke 16) is a vivid reminder that outward appearances don't provide a good basis for judging spirituality. If someone is truly suffering in punishment for sin, that person will likely know it without our saying a word. If that person doesn't realize it, it is still probably better to ask him what he thinks God is saying through the affliction, rather than offering our opinion that he must have committed some sin. If someone is suffering for righteousness' sake, as was Job, it definitely won't help if those who aren't suffering assume an attitude of moral superiority and accuse the sufferer of sin.

"This has probably spared you from worse problems."

Sometimes when we lose a loved one, people try to comfort us by convincing us that what has happened is for the best because it spares us from other problems. Here I relate the experience of one of my students. He was in my class during the term when he and his wife had their first baby. About midway through the term, the baby died very suddenly. After the funeral and toward the end of our class sessions, he shared with the class some of what he had learned. Part of what he told us focused on what not to say to someone experiencing such grief. He told us how some people had said, "You know, it's probably good that your son died. He probably would have grown up to be a problem. Maybe he'd have been a drug addict or would have refused to follow Christ. God knows these things in advance, and he is probably just saving you from those problems."

I trust that no one thinks this is an appropriate thing to say. It may be true that the child *would* have been a problem, but it is hard to see how that information is a comfort at the time of loss. Parents and other relatives love that child, and they love him regardless of whether or not he was or would have been a problem. The loss is extremely painful, and the pain is not eased, let alone removed, by insensitive speculations about the future. Moreover, the comment is wrong, because it in effect says that it

41

is good that evil has happened. I don't see how that can ever be an appropriate attitude for a Christian. Yes, James says we are to count it all joy when we fall into various afflictions (James 1:1–2), but we must not misunderstand this. The affliction isn't joy; it is evil. The cause for joy is that in spite of the evil, God is with us, comforts us, and can accomplish positive things in our lives even in the midst of affliction. But the affliction isn't a good thing. If it were, we might be inclined to seek suffering. Obviously, nothing in Scripture suggests that we should do that. Anyway, we don't have to seek affliction; it will find us.

"Just remember Romans 8:28."

It is not unusual for some well-meaning person to see us suffering and offer the following advice. "I can see this is quite a struggle for you. But just remember that in Romans 8:28 God promises that all things work together for good." Though quoting Scripture to the afflicted can be a good strategy, there are a number of reasons why quoting this passage is not necessarily helpful.

First, those who understand what you are saying usually remember that there is more to the verse. Paul says that this will happen to "those who love [God], who have been called according to his purpose." It is possible that reminding sufferers of this verse will stir up in them a variety of doubts. They may reason, "Since all things work together for good for those who love God and are called according to his purpose, maybe the reason that this is happening and hasn't yet turned out for good is that my love for God isn't what it should be. Or maybe God has his will and purposes for me, but I'm out of his will, and that's why this has happened. In fact, maybe by quoting this verse my friend is implicitly accusing me of those problems." Surely, such doubts in no way help the sufferer. The would-be comforter of course doesn't intend to make the burden heavier by adding a burden of doubt and guilt.

Second, Paul is clearly appealing to the ability of a sovereign God to turn everything that happens to believers, even adversity, into something profitable for them. But in light of verses 29–30, which explain why verse 28 is true, it is clear that the good envisioned here pertains to the believer's salvation, not just anything that contributes to worldly convenience or comfort. Paul writes: "For those God foreknew he also predestined to be conformed to the likeness of his Son, that he might be the firstborn among many brothers. And those he predestined, he also called; those he called, he also justified; those he justified, he also glorified."

Nonetheless, those who quote this verse often think it guarantees a life of ease and convenience. If it doesn't, it is simply misleading to quote this verse as though it means that the afflicted should feel better because God will soon restore what we lost that made life simple and easy for us. That surely is not the verse's point.

Third, reminding the sufferer of Romans 8:28, especially in the early stages of the sufferer's affliction, treats what is primarily an emotional problem as though it is only an intellectual one. We think that if we can just get the sufferer the "right" information, all the pain will go away. If the mother of the little girl who skinned her knee quoted Romans 8:28 to her daughter, would that remove the pain? Of course not, and not just because she's a little girl.

Do not misunderstand this. There will be a time in the sufferer's experience when it will be helpful to offer this and other biblical and theological information in an attempt to comfort (see the appendix). But when emotional and physical pain are so severe, don't expect the sufferer's mind to be functioning at full speed. Even if it is, the right information won't remove the pain!

There are two final problems with quoting this verse, and I think these are the most significant. Fourth, at the point in our suffering when someone quotes this verse, God typically hasn't brought good out of this evil. Often those who suffer can't see how or when God will do so. Reminding them of what God can do before God has done anything isn't likely to help very much.

And fifth, it is hard to see how that good, whenever it comes and whatever it will be, will make up for the evil that has happened. Surely, the would-be comforter does not mean to say that the evil that has happened is really all right because eventually God will overrule this adversity to do something good! Moreover, I hope that by quoting this verse no one is suggesting that since God will turn things to good, even the evil that has happened isn't really evil! Unfortunately, quoting Romans 8:28 may just give the sufferer such false impressions. How insensitive to imply that a tragedy of a lost loved one, or some other tragedy, really isn't that bad or that it isn't even evil at all, because God will eventually bring something good out of the experience. God used the murder of Jesus Christ on Calvary to purchase our salvation, but that doesn't make our Lord's death any less a murder, nor does it mean that those who put him to death deserve praise as moral heroes!

Remember that even Jesus wept when Lazarus died (John 11:35). The fact that Jesus had power to raise his friend from the dead (and did so) didn't cause Jesus to think that what had happened was trivial. Jesus knew this was a terrible evil, and so he wept, even though he knew he could raise Lazarus from the dead. Scripture also tells us that as a result of sin, the whole creation was subjected to frustration (Rom. 8:20). The fact that God will someday reverse the curse placed on creation (Rom. 8:21) in no way minimizes the evil that has happened. God's overturning the results of sin in our world and using that to demonstrate his glory and power don't mean the sin was good. After all, God told the human race not to sin. The fact that he can display his mighty and gracious hand in saving sinners does not mean he is actually happy that we sinned, making his salvation possible, or that sin is not really sin.

Things happen in our world that really *are* evil! Don't minimize that fact by appealing to the sovereign ability of God to bring good even out of the most horrible situation. Somewhere down the road, after the sufferer's pain has somewhat subsided and there has been time to see what God will do in the midst of the tragedy, maybe then it will be a comfort to remind the sufferer of this verse. But don't be surprised if the afflicted person has already recited that verse many times over. Regardless of what good God has brought out of the evil situation, that doesn't mean the evil isn't really evil. And quoting this verse, true though it is, won't make the pain go away.

"We're all going to die someday."

Not long after we learned the truth about my wife's condition, someone said to me, "Well, you know, everyone's going to die from something. You just know in advance what it is in your wife's case."

Even if this is true, how can it be a comfort? Does the thought of your own death bring you comfort? If you knew in advance the *cause* of your own death, would you be inclined to say, "Ah, well, very good; now I can rest easy knowing what will get me"? No one likes to reflect on their own or a loved one's demise. That it will happen to all of us is no encouragement, nor is knowing the manner of our death. That is true even if ours will be an "easy death," much less facing death from a catastrophic disease. At the time of someone's grief, do not think you will help him by reminding him that we will all die someday, or that at least he knows in advance how he will die.

The other problem with this comment is that it is not necessarily true—that is, we can never know in advance the exact cause of our death. Indeed, the likelihood that my wife will die of Huntington's disease is great, but it isn't absolutely certain. She could die of a heart attack, in a car accident, or some other way. None of that is cause for rejoicing either, but it does show that the comment about knowing how one will die is neither helpful nor necessarily correct.

Furthermore, it doesn't help to remind me or my wife that despite her disease and despite the fact that it takes people when they are relatively young, I might still die before she does. That could also be true, but I don't find it comforting to think that at a time when Pat is least able to function and most in need of my help, I might not be there. That doesn't encourage her either.

"Don't think about any major changes."

When the doctor first diagnosed Pat's condition, he made some statements that he must have thought would be helpful. After giving the diagnosis, he said, "Well, you better think about it long and hard before having any more children. And, you and your husband better not think about changing jobs. If you do, you might not be able to get health insurance."

I am confident that her physician meant well by offering this practical advice. Indeed, we needed to think about these issues. But there is a time to be told such things, and right at the outset isn't it. Earlier I described the feelings of abandonment and hopelessness. Along with those feelings is the sense that one is trapped in the situation and helpless to escape. What that doctor said in no way helped to alleviate those feelings. On the contrary, his words confirmed our feelings of entrapment. While I love my job and where I'm doing it, nobody likes to feel that their life's options are being limited or cut off, especially when they face seemingly insurmountable problems.

Yes, we needed that information, but not at that time. When someone you know gets shocking news, they are in need of some practical advice about their situation. However, timing is crucial. I would encourage you to be ultrasensitive to their feelings. At the moment when they are feeling totally devastated by the news, don't add to their misery by telling them things that will only add to their feelings of entrapment and abandonment. If you feel you must say something, it would probably be better just to encourage them not to make any major decisions until they've had some time to sort things out. But they probably know that already.

"I know how you feel."

One of the most typical statements people make is something I myself have said at times when visiting the sick or bereaved. As we fumble for something to share that will comfort our friend or loved one, somehow it seems appropriate to say: "I know how you must feel at a time like this." Through my experiences, I have learned how inappropriate and unhelpful this comment can be. The problem is really twofold. On the one hand, it isn't true, and the sufferer knows it. Hence, it sounds phony when you say it. Even if you think you know how I feel, and even if the same thing happened to you, you still don't know how I feel and you can't know how I feel! You can't because you are not me with my particular personality and emotions, with my background and experiences, with my family and the relations we share with one another. Nor can I know exactly how *you* feel when suffering comes your way. Telling me that you know how I feel sounds like an insincere and cheap way to try to comfort me. I know it can't be true.

If something similar has indeed happened to you, you may tell me this because you think I might be encouraged by hearing that others have suffered greatly and yet have survived. If that is your point, then just say that, rather than saying you know how I feel. What you say may still not comfort me, because I may be in too much pain at the time to think I'll ever make it through the particular crisis at hand. You can say this from the vantage point of looking back at your own crisis and seeing that you survived. But remember, I'm still in the midst of my crisis. Your experience is no guarantee that I'll make it.

While your reassurance that you and others have survived tragedy may not comfort me, at least that comment is true. You aren't telling me you know how I feel when I know you can't know how I feel. You are simply saying that though these things are hard, others like yourself have experienced tragedy and have survived. Unless I am totally different from everyone else, it is possible for me to make it too.

The other problem with saying you know how I feel is that it really doesn't matter whether you know how I feel. Do you think I would rejoice in knowing that you feel as miserable as I do? I wouldn't wish my feelings of grief on my enemies, let alone my friends. To know that you feel as bad as I do would make me feel worse, not better. Beyond that, the fundamental reason it doesn't matter whether or not you know how I feel is that this information alone won't help me. What helps is not knowing you feel like I do, but knowing that you care!

Look at it this way. Suppose some horrible tragedy happened to you. Suppose I had experienced the same thing, and suppose I know you. Imagine that I tell you, "I know exactly how you feel. I've been there myself. But you know what? While I know how you feel, I don't really care about what's happening to you."

Would that comfort or help you? Of course not. However, if I tell you I *don't* know how you feel, but I *do* care, and I want to be of help, that will make a difference. It will especially help if your words are followed by tangible deeds that show you are serious about helping. Remember, those who suffer feel helpless, hopeless, and abandoned. They need us to care and to show that care by helping any way we can. *They don't need us to share their feelings; they need us to share their burdens!*

Here I must also add that it doesn't really help to tell me that Jesus knows how I feel, because he suffered greatly during his earthly pilgrimage. Or that God knows how I feel about losing Pat, because he watched his Son die on Calvary. I take no comfort from any of that. Rather my reaction is: "Oh great. Just what we need—more victims. This is definitely not a time when misery wants company!" The fact that God himself has suffered because of the sin of the human race in no way encourages or comforts me. It reminds me of my part in making his suffering necessary, and that only makes me feel worse.

I have found 1 Peter 5:7 to be a very helpful passage. But it is important to see what this familiar passage *doesn't* say as well as what it does say. Peter could have written, "Cast all your cares upon him, because he has suffered too, and knows how you feel." I find that statement to be nowhere near as encouraging as what Peter did write. Peter tells us to cast our cares on Christ, because he *cares* for us. That's the key. Not someone to feel as bad as we do, but someone who cares about our troubles and is there to help carry our burdens.

In all of this, it is very important to recognize the difference between "I know how you feel" and "I really feel for you." The former identifies with the sufferer. The latter shows we care.

"If you'd just change your view of God, everything would be fine."

The months wore on after my wife's diagnosis, and I longed to have someone to talk to about how I felt. A dear, godly colleague who has been a friend for many years offered to listen. I began to explain how perplexed I was by what had happened. It seemed that God hid information from us about my wife prior to our marriage, and again prior to our having children. I noted that with my Calvinistic conception of God, where God controls all things, this was especially troublesome. Even if I were more inclined toward an Arminian notion of God, where God takes a less active role in the world to leave more room for human freedom, it still seemed to me that God should have intervened in our behalf. After all, hadn't we prayed that the Lord would lead us and keep us from making a wrong decision about whether to marry? My friend replied that I was talking about this concept of God and that model of God; what I really needed to do was stop such talk and recognize that God is bigger than all our conceptions of him.

There is something very right about what my friend said. Surely we can never hope to understand thoroughly our majestic and mighty God through human thought forms. Yet I found my friend's comments unhelpful. For one thing, he failed to see that his comment about God being bigger than all our conceptions of him is itself another conception of God.

However, the real problem was that my friend in essence was saying that things would be better for me if I just changed my ideas about God. Now it is true that sufferers who are atheists need to change their perception of God. A Christian who has little training in theology might also need a better understanding of the nature and attributes of God. In fact, even theology professors from time to time could stand to adjust their views to a more accurate picture of God.

But even though this is true, there is still a major problem in thinking that this will resolve the religious problem of evil. What is wrong with telling someone suffering greatly that all they really need to do is just change their view of God? The problem is that this treats a fundamentally emotional problem as if it were an intellectual problem. Please do not misunderstand this. The afflicted *may* have a wrong concept of God, and at some point in dealing with them, we must help them get a better picture of what God is like. On the other hand, if the religious problem of evil is, as I suggest, at root an emotional hurt, that must be handled first. You don't handle an emotional problem by telling someone to adjust her idea of God. You can change your view of God and still find that the pain remains!

There are other forms of this error that are just as common among Christians. One is, "You know, if you were a Calvinist, you'd see that God is in control of all of this, and then you could rest in him." Another is, "You know, if you weren't so Calvinistic, you wouldn't think God has his hand so directly in everything, and then you'd stop blaming him for what's happened to you." Perhaps the most common is, "When things like this happen, aren't you glad you're a Calvinist? Isn't it great to know that God is ultimately in control of it all, and that he's already planned the way out of your problem?"

The first two of these comments are really saying that this whole situation will be all right if you just change your view of God. We have already talked about this mistake. The third comment doesn't tell sufferers to get a new concept of God but rather tells them to take comfort in their beliefs about God. Don't assume, though, that this will actually comfort everyone. I am a Calvinist, and I found this comment distressing, not helpful. Because of my belief in God's control over all things, and because it appeared that God had misled me, I took no comfort in the fact that I was a Calvinist. In fact, I remember thinking quite frequently that everything that had happened to me and my family would be easier to take if I were an Arminian. At least then I wouldn't see God so actively and directly in control of what had happened.

What was the problem here? Was it that I really needed to discard my Calvinism as inadequate? Not at all. Had I been an Arminian, what had happened would still hurt terribly. The problem was that others who made the comment, and I as well, thought this deep emotional wound could be salved by simply reflecting on this intellectual concept. Indeed, there is a time for explanation and reflection upon what one knows to be true of God. If one's ideas about God are wrong, there is also a time for changing them. But not when the hurt is so deep and so new!

Remember the little girl with the skinned knee. In answer to her mother's explanations she says, "Yes, Mommy, but it still hurts." This is not a problem that requires philosophical or theological discourse; it requires pastoral care. In any given case, no one can predict how long it will take for the pain to subside to the point where the sufferer is ready to think seriously about concepts of God. You can be sure, however, that until it does, it won't help the afflicted to tell them to change their view of God or to simply meditate on what they believe about him.

"You aren't spiritually mature unless you're happy about this."

In the midst of this emotional and spiritual turmoil and upheaval, I was also concerned about my response to our situation, and I felt guilty that I wasn't on top of things. After all, Christians are supposed to rejoice in all things and persevere no matter what. Beyond that, as one in a position of Christian leadership, people would be looking all the more closely at me to see how I handled this. Still, I was finding it hard to cope. I preach quite frequently, but for about six months I was physically, emotionally, and spiritually unable to do so. I felt that anything I would say would be hypocritical because I wasn't living whatever I might preach.

All of this was disturbing enough, but my uneasiness increased. One day I was listening to a Christian radio program. A husband and wife who had lost a daughter in her twenties in an automobile accident were giving their testimony. They recounted what had happened to their daughter and how, as a result of these events, various people had come to know the Lord. They concluded that even though the loss of their daughter was hard, it was all for the best. It was good that this had happened.

I heard that and I felt more guilty. It seemed the height of Christian maturity to take life's harshest blows and say that it was good that this had happened. If that's what it means to be victorious in the midst of affliction, I knew I was far from that. I couldn't rejoice over the evil that had befallen and would befall my family. But wasn't I supposed to? After all, doesn't Paul tell us to "give thanks in all circumstances, for this is God's will for you in Christ Jesus" (1 Thess. 5:18)? My sense of inadequacy increased.

What my friend and colleague said on this matter was most helpful. I told him I knew I was supposed to respond Christianly in this situation. Did that mean, though, that I had to like what was happening? Without batting an eyelash he responded, "You do have to learn to live with this, but that doesn't mean you have to like it!"

This may sound like heresy to some. Popular Christian belief reminds us to rejoice in everything and count it all joy when trials come our way. One is not really "with it" spiritually without being able to say that the affliction is a good thing—or so we are told. I beg to differ. Thinking that way won't help us to cope with our grief; it will only add to it as we feel guilty about our inability to do what we think we are called to do.

My friend was right, and I came to see why as I reflected on this over the following weeks and months. First Thessalonians 5:18 is often misread. Paul does not say that we are to give thanks *for* everything, but *in* everything (that is, in the midst of everything). The affliction is evil, not good. Why should I thank God for evil? Furthermore, James 1:2–4 does not say that affliction is good or that it is a cause for rejoicing. It says that we are to rejoice when these things happen because God is sufficient in the midst of trials. We are to rejoice when we face trials because we can see what God is accomplishing *in spite of* the trials. Affliction may serve as the occasion for God to do good things in our life, but the suffering is not good. It is still evil.

Because the affliction is evil, I am not required to like it. All of us have sinned, and so we live in a fallen world. That is why it is even possible for these tragedies to happen. Scripture is very clear that people die because of sin (Rom. 5:12). If people are going to die, they must die from something, and many will die from diseases that take life. Unless Jesus Christ returns for his church before we die, all of us will die as a consequence of living in a fallen world. Please do not misunderstand this. I am not suggesting that the reason Pat has Huntington's disease is that she is a much worse sinner than others and this is her just punishment. On the contrary, I would contend that she is far more godly than most people I have ever known. My point is that all of us have sinned, and hence we are all responsible for the fallen world in which we live.

If disease and death are ultimately the consequences of living in a sinful, fallen world, how can I applaud it? As a Christian, I am called to resist sin and its consequences in all forms. How then can I exult when the consequences of sin befall anyone, let alone a loved one? No, we don't have to like it, and if we properly understand the ultimate cause of disease and death, we had better not like it!

It is wrong in another respect to suggest that the sufferer give thanks for suffering; it is wrong because it ignores our humanness. Grief and sorrow in the face of tragedy are very human emotions. Unless they are admitted and expressed, they will remain inside us and destroy us. Healing can't come if we deny what we are feeling and act as though it is good that evil has happened. Those negative feelings must be admitted and expressed. They must be dealt with, not hidden so that the sufferer *acts* as though everything is all right. We can't help the afflicted if we expect them to deny their humanness. Realizing that I didn't have to like what was happening relieved a great burden.

"Time heals all wounds, so you must be all right by now."

As Pat's disease has worn on, something further has happened that I never anticipated. And it is in no way helpful. Over the weeks, months, and years of dealing with tragedy, people who suffer "get used" to the problem they are facing. Adjustments in schedules are made as needed, and after a while, life returns to at least a semblance of normality.

As this happens, those dealing with suffering and trials speak less often about the challenges facing them. Friends and family tend to take this as a cue that the sufferer is getting over whatever horrible things have happened. They assume, then, that the afflicted person must be doing fine with what has happened. As a result, they make little point to ask about the situation or offer any help that might be needed. Since the sufferer isn't mentioning the problems, friends and family seem to act as though they believe the old adage—time heals all wounds—must be true of the one suffering. It would follow, then, that friends would resume their friendship with the afflicted person, and that the relationship would be more like it was before tragedy struck. But often that doesn't happen. Having gotten into a habit of staying away from the sufferer, they continue to do so, assuming that there is no longer any need for comfort or help. Or perhaps they stay away because there is still a lingering fear that the sufferer may want to talk about their loss, and the friend will be inadequate to respond to whatever might be said.

Such attitudes are not helpful at all. There is a sense in which one never gets over a tragic loss. Oh, the intense pain that was there when tragedy first struck is gone, but don't think what has happened doesn't still hurt. Continuing to remain at a distance communicates to the afflicted that you have forgotten entirely about his situation and think he is fine; or that you do think about the sufferer's hardships but you just don't care enough to get involved to see how he is doing, how he feels, and how you can help; or that you sense your friend is having a struggle but you don't want to get involved for fear that you might not say the right thing.

Though such attitudes and reactions toward the sufferer can occur, reject them. Don't use such views to rationalize not extending comfort and encouragement to the afflicted! Giving the impression that you think the sufferer is "all right" only makes him or her feel more abandoned; it communicates that friends don't understand how painful things still are, and that they think the sufferer needs no further comfort, encouragement, and help. But that's wrong. The burdens the sufferer bears are just as heavy as they ever were, and after bearing them for a long time, in some ways they hurt even more than they did at the start. Please remember, personal tragedy leaves an indelible mark that will only go away in eternity when God wipes away all tears. But we aren't there yet; so while the sufferer still bears the loss (as will be the case as long as he or she lives), continue to minister to his or her needs, just as you did during the first days, months, and years after tragedy struck.

The list of unhelpful comments discussed in this chapter is not exhaustive, but I hope you will think deeply about them. However, please don't let a fear that you might say or do something "wrong" keep you from being with and ministering to the afflicted!

In chapter 2, I mentioned that when tragedy strikes, friends often leave the afflicted alone, because they are afraid that they will say something wrong to make the situation worse. Or they may fear that they won't have something profound to say that will relieve the pain. All of this underscores a basic misjudging of what the sufferer really needs. When tragedy first strikes, and for a long time after, the bereaved need some way to express all the thoughts and feelings they are experiencing. They long to have someone who cares enough just to listen to them pour out their heart. Though it is natural to want to say something that will relieve the sufferer's pain, it is even more important that we listen to what they want to say.

In the next chapters I turn to those things that did help me. They didn't all happen at once, and in some cases it took awhile after they occurred for their import to sink in. If you are wrestling with the religious problem of evil, I trust that you will read these chapters with that in mind.

THE GOODNESS OF GOD

Grace for Today

Amidst all the unhelpful remarks and actions, one thing that did help over time came in a conversation with my father several weeks after we first received Pat's diagnosis. I was bemoaning the fact that things looked so hopeless. I couldn't see how I would be able to handle it as Pat got worse. On top of that, there was the prospect of having to go through the same thing with one or more of our children. I didn't know how I would make it. At that point Dad said, "John, God never promised to give you tomorrow's grace for today. He only promised today's grace for today, and that's all you need!"

How true that is! In that one comment I was reminded both of God's grace and of my need to take each day one at a time. God has impressed upon me the fact that I don't have to live my tomorrows today. I don't know how I'll cope when my tomorrows come, but I know that they will come only one day at a time, and with each day, even as now, there will be grace to meet each new challenge—for me and for my wife. That doesn't mean it will be fun, but it does mean that for each day God will provide the strength needed.

I have always been a goal-oriented person with an eye to planning for the future. As a result of this truth about grace, I began to readjust my focus from the future to the present. I would begin each day asking God for just the grace needed to sustain me that day. As that prayer was answered day after day, I gained more assurance that God would be there when things got worse. As a result, I found that I worried less about the future and focused more on the present day and its responsibilities. I still think about and plan for the future, but increasingly as Pat's condition has worsened, I think in terms of the near future.

Often people ask me whether I am a member of a Huntington's disease support group. Some of them have addresses, phone numbers, and email information to help me get involved. I know that such groups can be very helpful and that they are truly a lifeline for many families. I am not in such a group, however, and that is by choice. My personality is such that if I saw other Huntington's patients and heard them and their families talk about their challenges, I would likely project their symptoms and struggles onto our own situation. That would not be wise at all. While there is a group of symptoms associated with Huntington's disease, no one can predict which symptoms will afflict each person, nor is it clear how long any symptom will last or how severe it will be. Because of the nature of this disease—and it has taken an unpredictable path in Pat's case—I see no reason to worry about symptoms she may never have. Jesus told us not to worry about tomorrow's problems today (Matt. 6:34), and that makes abundant sense. I don't have tomorrow's grace now, so I'm not ready for its problems either. And I especially shouldn't worry about tomorrow's problems when those challenges may never include symptoms other Huntington's patients have. So while being in a support group works well for others, I have taken a different path.

Over the years as Pat's condition has gotten worse, I have followed the same basic approach. Of course, I have to plan for her future needs. That became especially clear as I gradually became less able to care for her in the home. I dreaded the day that I might have to move her into a nursing home, but I couldn't just sit back and wait until that day came to find out how to do that and which nursing home would be best. Even now, I still handle Pat's situation best when I focus on her daily needs and on details that will need to be addressed in the near future. If I were to look at everything at once that must be done over a period of years of dealing with this disease, it looks like an impossible task. But when I focus just on the immediate needs, the situation is not so insurmountable. And, I can say now, over twenty-eight years since we first received Pat's diagnosis, that God has faithfully provided grace for each day and each challenge! I have no doubt that his grace will be there every day for the rest of our lives.

The Importance of Listening

In the weeks and months following Pat's diagnosis, I had so many thoughts and emotions rushing through my mind that I felt like there was a war going on inside my head. I felt like I would explode if I couldn't share what I was feeling. I needed to express my thoughts, but I found few who would listen. It's not that I think friends and acquaintances didn't really care. I just think they weren't sure what to expect if they listened and whether they might make me feel worse by saying the wrong thing in response to what I would say. It was easier to pray for us or to offer a word of concern than to listen. Even today there are times when I just need someone to listen to how I feel and to what I've been thinking. And this is why it is so important for us to "be there" to listen, even if we have nothing profound to say in response. At times of crises our profoundest contribution is our presence and our open ears. It says that we care and we understand the need to make public what is going on inside the sufferer's head and heart.

So don't avoid the afflicted out of fear that you don't have the "magic words" to make the pain go away. Even if you have those words, when the pain is new and so intense, the sufferer cannot process what you would say. By listening instead, you gain the right to be heard when the sufferer is really ready and able to listen. Those who won't listen when listening is needed communicate either that they don't care about what the sufferer is feeling and thinking, or that they have the ready answer to the problem and thus what has happened must not be all that bad. Unwittingly, they communicate that they don't really understand or fully appreciate what the sufferer is experiencing.

In the book of Job, we see these points vividly illustrated. Job's friends made a lot of mistakes in "ministering" to his needs, but one thing they did was exactly what he needed. After the second wave of afflictions, Job's friends came to comfort him, and they sat with him for seven days and nights. *And they said nothing.* Scripture says that they didn't speak to him because they saw that his grief was very great (Job 2:13). This showed great sensitivity to how he was feeling and to what would most help him. We are not told what Job said or did during those seven days and nights. But surely his friends were right to be there and to be quiet! The trouble began when they opened their mouths, attempting to soothe his grief by dumping upon him a load of speculations about why this had happened and what he should do to relieve his pain.

God's timing in responding to Job also illustrates this point. Job repeatedly sought God and expressed his wish to plead his case before God. "Oh that I knew where I might find Him," says Job, "that I might come to His seat! I would present my case before Him and fill my mouth with arguments" (Job 23:3–4 NASB). Yet God remained silent.

God could have spoken the words recorded in chapters 38–41

shortly after Job's afflictions began, but he didn't. Some may reply that if God's answer had come immediately after chapter 2, it would ruin the literary impact of the book. Only after we read the many chapters of dialogue between Job and his friends are we ready to hear God's answer. I would not discount this point about the literary form of dialogue or about the impact of placing these chapters where the author did. But there is no indication that this is a fictional story in which the author could have imagined the events in any sequence that would fit his literary agenda. Instead, the author is telling us that God really waited a long time before he answered Job.

And that makes abundant sense, for surely God knows our nature far better than we do. Thus, he knew that what Job needed was time and opportunity to express his feelings, his questions, and his doubts. And so God kept silent, listening to Job vent his thoughts and emotions. God is too wise to think that had he spoken the words of chapters 38–41 right after the afflictions fell, Job would have been ready to hear and process them. It was only after Job had repeatedly thought through his situation and stated his feelings again and again that he was ready to hear God's reply. And so God waited, listening not speaking. We would be wise to do the same as we minister to the afflicted.

Job wanted to find God so that he could plead his case before him. Though Job didn't sense it, God was actually there all the time, listening to Job and his friends. And he is present in our lives when we experience the pain of tragedy. We wish that he would explain why this is happening to us, but God listens to our expressions of grief, waiting to answer us at just the moment when we are ready to hear him.

In my case, I needed listeners. Friends who listened to me ministered much more than I even realized at the time. I can't imagine how much harder this experience would have been if no one had listened. One of those who did listen was a professional counselor. I remember that I had certain expectations about what would happen in the sessions with him. I didn't expect him to answer all my theological and philosophical questions about what was happening. But I did expect him to tell me what to do to move beyond the deep grief I was feeling. Much to my surprise (and, to a certain extent, frustration), he said very little in any of our sessions, especially the early ones. He asked an occasional question to keep me talking about my thoughts and feelings, but he offered little advice or commentary.

Early on, I thought that the sessions were somewhat a waste of time, because I was taking from them so little that seemed helpful. On the other hand, I thought to myself that at least now I was getting a chance to lay out in detail piece by piece my thoughts and feelings about what was happening. And, even if he had little advice to offer, at least getting the chance to say what I was thinking was good. As the sessions continued, the counselor began to give some advice, and I found it helpful. Because he had listened so patiently to me, how could I not listen carefully to him? Moreover, I knew that whatever advice he offered was given from the vantage point of one who had a thorough knowledge of my thoughts and feelings. There would be little need to counter what he said by adding elements of my story that might change his advice. He already knew many of the details because he had listened so well.

I have devoted much space to this point, because I think it so important. Listening alone won't make the pain go away, but it is a key first step. I hope I can encourage readers not to abandon the sufferer. I hope you will see that even if you don't have something to say that will remove the pain, you should still go to your suffering friend or family member. This is true not only when tragedy first strikes; it is true for as long as the sufferer deals with his loss. Even now, there are times when I just need someone to listen to me talk about how I feel and what I think about what is happening to my wife and family. Listening is far more helpful than you can ever imagine.

The Importance of Visiting the Sick and Grieving

Here I must add that it is important for others to visit people who are sick. Thankfully, there are some friends who visit Pat regularly. But others visited only occasionally, and then stopped once Pat was not able to talk or interact with them. I understand that people like to think that when they visit the sick, it makes a difference to the patient. When the patient can't respond, it is easy to think you are accomplishing nothing, and so I understand why they stop visiting. But I must say two things. If you go at least in part because you think you can do some good for the patient, don't assume you haven't helped just because the patient can't speak. If you could not speak, would you be happy to be left alone all day? Not being able to speak does not mean she cannot notice what is happening around her, nor does it mean your visit counts for nothing!

The other point is that if you go because doing so makes you feel good about being a caring person who visits the sick, and if you think the only way to know that you've helped is if the patient interacts with you, that is the wrong approach. Visiting the sick is not about making visitors feel better about themselves. It must be about making things better for the patient. But, how, with a disease such as Pat's, can I do anything to make her situation better, you may wonder. You make things better by showing her that even though her abilities are diminished and she can contribute little or nothing to a conversation (or to anything else), there are still people who love her and care about her, anyway. If family members of the patient feel that they are abandoned with this intolerable burden of caring for a slowly dying relative, how much more hopeless, helpless, and useless must the person with the disease feel! Nobody wants to be a burden or to place a heavy burden on those who care for her. If you abandon your sick friend, what does that communicate? Does it say that now because things are getting more hopeless, you no longer care about them and feel comfortable discarding them? Does it mean that because you no longer see any signs that your visit has helped, there is no reason to visit? Surely, visiting the sick is not about making us feel better about ourselves for having spent time with someone who can do so little; visiting must be about helping to make life more enjoyable, even if only for a short time, for the person dealing with the disease.

Please do not misunderstand this. I have not written these things to make anyone feel guilty for not visiting the sick or to make anyone feel obligated. My point is rather to affirm that your visit does matter, even if the sick person cannot tell you how much it does. And I am writing this to encourage you to visit and to keep your focus on what your visit will do for the sick person, not on how good it might make you feel about yourself.

The Importance of Tangible Care

Another major factor in helping me to cope, though I didn't realize it at the time, was seeing that God and others really do care. This was especially so during the first months and years of dealing with this disease. I wrote in previous chapters of the sense of abandonment and helplessness one feels. It seems that an incredible burden has been put on one's shoulders, and no one is there to help carry it. In the midst of those feelings, God used various people to show me that he and others knew what my wife and I were going through—and that they cared.

Several incidents were especially meaningful. Shortly after we learned the news about Pat, my brother came to encourage me. I remember him saying that though I might feel abandoned at that moment, God hadn't abandoned me, and neither had he or the rest of my family. At that point I was still in such shock that I didn't recognize that I was actually feeling a sense of abandonment. But God knew it, and sent my brother to reassure me.

I also remember an important visit from my pastor. No one told him to visit us, and we hadn't asked that he come. He knew we were hurting, and he cared enough to do something. I remember well the first thing he said to me. He told me that he couldn't begin to know how I felt, but he wanted me to know that he really cared about what was happening, and that he and the church wanted to help in any way possible. I didn't realize it, but I really needed to hear that. He didn't say much more, but he was willing to be there and listen. His presence said he cared. At a time when it seems impossible to survive the grief and when everything appears hopeless, we need to know that someone cares and will help.

There were other visits, and words were matched with actions. My pastor noticed that our home was in need of some decorating. He took it upon himself to get together a group of people from the church to do it. It was their way of saying they loved us, were sorry about what had happened, and wanted to do something tangible to express that love. Some might think this was a strange thing for them to do. After all, how could painting some rooms help with this catastrophic disease? On the contrary, however, what they did struck me as God's way of showing me that if these people cared enough to do this, they and others would also be there when I needed more involved help to care for my wife. People feel so bad about what is happening, and they just wish that they could do something tangible to express their love and concern. Let them do things like my church friends did. It will be good for them and for you! As Pat's condition has deteriorated and she is able to do less, Christian friends and acquaintances are still there showing in various ways that they care. What a beautiful picture of God's love for us!

What my pastor and church did in our home illustrates another point about caring for the afflicted. Often when we hear of someone in need, we tell them, "If there's anything I can do to be of help, just let me know." This expresses concern, but think about what else it does. On top of all the grief and pain the sufferer is feeling, he or she now has an assignment—devote some of your emotional and mental energy to thinking about something I can do for you. We can be smarter than this, can't we? We know that groceries need to be bought, children need to be taken to music lessons and team practices, lawns need to be mowed, and rooms need painting. Why not tell the afflicted, "I know Jimmy has baseball practice this afternoon, and I'd be happy to see that he gets there and back." Or, "I'm going to the grocery store this morning; can I pick up some fruit that's on a special sale now and some other groceries for you?" Or, "I can see that you have rooms in your home that haven't been painted in a long time. Let me organize a group of friends to come and do that for you."

All of these imagined comments have at least one thing in common. They mention a specific need and a way that you would be happy to fill it. That way, rather than offering unspecific help in general, the sufferer knows that you really would like to do this. If you just offer help in general, the afflicted may be afraid to ask for something specific because it might not be something you'd really like to do or be able to do. Still, having offered, you'd be obligated to do it, even if you don't want to. Knowing this, my reaction when someone offers help in general is not to ask for anything, since I don't want to burden anyone with something they'd rather not do. But if you offer to do something specific, it saves me the time and effort of having to think up something you can do for me. Plus, if I agree to let you do this, I know I'm not asking you to do something you can't or don't want to do. Moreover, your offer of something specific, like my pastor did, tells me that you really do care and are attentive to my specific situation. That alone, not to mention the specific help you actually give me, encourages me greatly!

Not only have people at my church been helpful and caring, but so have colleagues and students at Trinity Evangelical Divinity School where I teach. After Pat was first diagnosed, students on their own initiative set aside special times each week to pray for us. Students and colleagues still pray for us and many in the Trinity community express their concern by asking periodically how we are doing and by offering help.

The administration at Trinity over the years has been wonderful in working with us and our situation. It was difficult for me to teach many of my classes for a long time after we received the news of Pat's Huntington's disease. Rather than scolding me or threatening to remove me from my teaching assignments, the administration responded with patience and understanding. I was scheduled for a sabbatical that first academic year when the news came, and I was supposed to work on some writing projects. But I was in such physical pain, not to mention emotional stress, that I didn't know how I would be able to write during my sabbatical. I mentioned this to the president and dean, suggesting that perhaps I should postpone the leave. They took a more compassionate approach. The president and board told me to take the quarter off, and to consider it a combination sabbatical and medical leave of absence. I was told not to worry about how much writing I would accomplish. Though I did in fact get much done that sabbatical, that didn't overshadow their care, concern, and compassion toward me at such a difficult time.

In more recent years as Pat's needs have grown and I have had to devote more time and attention to her care, Trinity's administration has been wonderfully gracious and helpful. They have willingly adjusted my schedule and responsibilities so that I can continue to minister at Trinity, and do so in a way that leaves me time to attend to Pat's needs. In fact, toward the end of the 1990s the provost and the dean noticed Pat's condition getting worse. In response, they took it upon themselves to draft a proposal that in essence lightened my teaching load and responsibilities on campus so that I could stay at home more of each week to care for Pat. Their proposal, however, did not even remotely suggest that my salary and benefits be reduced. As things turned out, I took on other responsibilities for the school so that I could be freer to attend to Pat's needs. But the kindness and concern shown by these administrators whose only desire was to help us manage our situation demonstrated vividly that those with whom I work not only say they care but also show that they do in tangible ways that are so very generous!

All these events and many more over the years have convinced me that there are people who actually care and will help us as Pat's condition requires it. I also view these acts of kindness as God's sign that he cares as well. All of this has ministered to me greatly and helped to overcome my feelings of abandonment, hopelessness, and helplessness. And I know who sends people to help us; God's care for us shines through the helpful deeds of others.

Evidence That God Cares

There is part of our story that I have only mentioned in passing, but it is worth elaborating in relation to this point about caring for the afflicted. In earlier chapters I mentioned my mother-in-law's chart from the hospital in New York where she spent the last decade of her life. Because she died ten years before Pat was diagnosed and because of our need to confirm or disconfirm the diagnosis in Pat's case, the hospital sent us the chart.

When the chart came, I began to look through it. My mother-in-law had been admitted to that hospital in 1967, five years before my wife and I met and married. As I read the chart, I didn't understand much of it, but one thing I saw horrified me. Within a few months of her arrival at the hospital, the diagnosis of Huntington's disease was recorded in her chart. The information that could have saved us from this situation was there for five years before I even met my wife. The information that could have kept us from having children and saddling them with this burden was right there from 1967 onward. It had been there for twenty years, and no one told us about it, even though we sought answers. When we finally did learn the truth, it wasn't from that chart.

When I saw that information, I was furious. You can see further why I was so angry and why I felt so cheated and misled. You can understand as well why comments about it being great to be a Calvinist at a time like this didn't comfort me but repulsed me.

In the months and years that have passed since that revelation, I have come to see this in a different way. For twenty years that information was there, and at any time we could have found it out. Why, then, did God not give it to us until 1987? As I wrestled with that question, I began to see his love and concern for us. God kept it hidden because he wanted me to marry Pat. She is a great woman and wife. My life would be so impoverished without her, but I probably would have missed that blessing had I known earlier. God wanted our three sons to be born. Each is a blessing and a treasure, but we would have missed that had we known earlier. God also knew that we needed to be in a community of brothers and sisters in Christ at church and at the seminary who would love us and care for us at this darkest hour, so he withheld that information, not because he accidently overlooked giving it to us and not because he is an uncaring, evil God who delights in seeing his children suffer. I have come to understand that he withheld it as a sign of his great care for us. There is never a good time to receive such news, but God knew that this was exactly the right time.

A Challenge to Keep Showing Care

I have written at length about the need to show those who suffer that we care, because I am convinced this is so very crucial. We must show those who are hurting that we really do care, not only by saying it, but also by showing it through our deeds. Above all, we must not avoid those who suffer. We must be there with them, even if only to listen. Your presence and willingness to listen and help say enough. They say you care. When we keep our distance from those who suffer, we confirm their worst fears that no one cares and no one will help. Show them that someone cares, not only when the initial shock comes, but in the weeks and months and years that follow. There is a sense in which one never completely recovers from tragedy. The need for the love and concern of others is always there.

Before I began my teaching ministry, I pastored a church for two years. My experiences in dealing with Pat's disease have impacted me greatly. If I were ever to pastor again, I know one thing I would definitely do. At the very outset, I would work with church leaders to identify all the people in the congregation with special needs. And I would see to it that at least once every week (and no less than once every two weeks) someone in the church would contact those people. It wouldn't always have to be the pastor, nor need it always be someone in a position of leadership who would do this. The main thing is that we check with these people to see how they are doing and to help meet their needs. People with special needs may have little or no contact whatsoever with anyone for weeks at a time. Your love and care for them may be the only thing that brings any light into their life and dispels their loneliness, and it may be the only reason that they continue on in the faith. Though it may seem like a small investment of time and energy to those who do help, there is no way you can imagine the positive impact it will make when those you serve see that someone still cares and is there to offer a helping hand.

Time doesn't heal some wounds—at least not completely. Even in cases where some healing has happened, the tragedy lives with the sufferer every day. Don't assume everything is all right just because the afflicted person isn't asking for prayer or other help day after day. Jesus hasn't abandoned that person; do what Jesus would do! Make your care for sufferers an integral part of your church's ministry!

Hope for the Future

In the weeks and months after Pat's diagnosis, I was vividly reminded about how difficult it is to go on with life without hope. I didn't really begin to feel much relief from my pain until I began to see some rays of hope. The fact that God and others cared was reason for hope, as was the realization that God would give grace for each new day. In addition, friends who knew about our situation and about this disease could point to specific reasons for hope. For one thing, research on this disease continues. With advances in genetic engineering in the area of gene therapy, there is reason for hope. It is possible that neither a cure nor even much help will come in time to aid my wife. Still there is reason for hope, because the disease in her case developed at first very slowly. In recent years her condition has deteriorated more rapidly, but she could be further along than she is. It is possible as well that in the next few years the deterioration might move more slowly again. Thankfully, research continues on this disease. Around the turn of the century, geneticists were able to figure out what the Huntington gene does to kill cells. Though they have not yet come up with a cure, at least they seem to have some ideas about how to combat this disease. That, of course, is good news for any of our children who may get this disease. Five to ten years could see significant advances in medical science.

Are these false hopes? I think not, but only time will tell. Even so, I believe it is crucial that people have some reason for hope. We must not offer false hope, but when there are legitimate grounds for hope we should be quick to point those out. Some of my colleagues are especially sensitive to this need. When a newspaper or journal article appears that chronicles some advance in research on Pat's disease, no matter how small or insignificant the development, they make a point to show me the article. They realize that it is difficult to go on without hope, so they bring these things to my attention.

God Is Good

Something else that helped me and continues to do so is focusing on the fact that in spite of what has happened, God is good.

One particular incident brought that very vividly to my attention. A little over a year after we first received news of my wife's condition, I was being considered for tenure where I teach. In the tenure review interview, I was asked a question that really stopped me in my tracks. One of the members of the committee asked, "In light of what you've been through, can you still say that God is good?" Though I answered affirmatively, I did so somewhat hesitantly. I realized that I had been focusing so much on the problems and on what God *hadn't* done that I really hadn't paid enough attention to all the evidence of his goodness in my life.

In the months that followed, I thought a lot about how many things were going well for us. I believe that no matter how much pain and turmoil one suffers, it helps the sufferer to focus on the ways that God has shown his goodness. Even if a situation seems absolutely terrible, upon reflection one can probably imagine ways for it to be worse. Counting one's blessings may seem trite, but it does in fact give a different perspective on one's encroaching troubles.

In our case, there were many evidences of God's goodness. For one thing, in its early stages the disease progressed very slowly. When doctors heard how long Pat had had symptoms, and when they saw where she was at the time, they found it hard to believe. Of course, in more recent years there has been significant deterioration, and there are no guarantees about the disease's future progression, but I can always be thankful for the many years of relative normality in my wife's condition. And even as we are now dealing with the disease in its advanced stages, I know (from some reading I've done) that there are terrible symptoms one can get with Huntington's, and yet we've never seen the worst of them in Pat's case. Dealing with this disease has been difficult, but I can always think of ways that it could have been worse! That those things have not happened is a sign of God's goodness to us.

In addition, the love and concern shown to us by other Christians continue, and periodically I am again reminded of God's goodness as I hear of people literally all over the world who have heard about this and are praying for us. In addition, I have often thought that it is a blessing to live at this time in history! During the early part of the twentieth century (let alone earlier), little was known about Huntington's. Now it is known that there is a physiological base to this disease, not a psychological one. As research has advanced, within the last fifteen to twenty years the chromosome and the exact genetic marker involved in this disease have been identified. And, as already noted, scientists and physicians continue to work on combating and perhaps even curing the disease. My wife could have lived at any other time in history and still had this disease. That she and our children live now we take as another sign of God's special goodness to us.

Then, while this disease is a major challenge, many other aspects of our lives are going very well. The Lord has allowed Pat and me to travel extensively throughout the world to minister in churches and Bible schools. Pat's last trip was in 2007, and I have taken only one ministry trip out of the country since then. Who would have imagined in 1987 when we received Pat's diagnosis that she would still be able to travel outside of the country for another twenty years? And my ministry at Trinity continues to be a great joy, and God has blessed us in many other areas of our lives. When I look at these things, I can truly say that God has been and is good to us. It is easy to focus on what is going wrong. But when you realize that we live in a world where Satan is so dominant and sin so rampant, it is amazing that anything ever goes right! The fact that many things do go right is ample evidence of God's grace and goodness to us. Surely we don't deserve it, and God isn't obligated to give it, but he does.

I am often reminded of 1 Peter 5:7 (already mentioned in chapter 3). That verse tells the reader to "cast all your anxiety on him because he cares for you." Usually we focus on the first part of that verse as we remind one another not to worry about what is happening. The latter part of the verse explains *why* we should do this, and I believe it is most instructive. Peter could have written, "Cast all your anxiety on him because he is powerful enough to do something about it." Or "because he knows the answer to your problems." Either of those thoughts would be just as true as what Peter wrote, but I'm glad Peter wrote what he did. It's as if he was saying, "Of course, he's powerful enough and intelligent enough to know and do something about our problems. He wouldn't be God if he weren't. What we want to know, though, is whether he cares enough to help us. And he does."

Indeed, God does care. Everywhere in our lives, in spite of what may be happening, we can find ample signs that God cares—if we only look for them. God cares because he is so good. Focusing on those truths, as well as reflecting on the many expressions of his goodness, won't entirely remove the pain and the doubts, but it can definitely help sufferers feel more comfortable with God. And that is more significant than you might imagine!

HIDING THE FUTURE

In spite of all these encouragements in the midst of affliction, there was still the nagging question of how this could have happened to us. After all, it is not just that my wife is a Christian and has given her life in service to the Lord. The question of why this should happen to her is especially nagging because it couldn't be God's retribution upon her for any sin she committed in her life. That she would get this disease was decided the moment she was conceived!

Be Angry at Sin

As I thought about that, I was reminded of an unpopular but very important biblical truth: things like this happen because we live in a fallen world. God told Adam and Eve that if they disobeyed him, they would die (Gen. 2:17). They disobeyed, and the curse fell on them. The apostle Paul reminds us that it fell on all of us as well (Rom. 5:12). Another way to say this is that Adam's sin and its consequences have been imputed or "credited" to the whole race. But if people die, they must die of something. There are many possible causes of death, and disease is one of them. Realizing this, one understands that though my wife committed no specific sin after birth that brought this disease upon her, this has in fact happened because of her sin in Adam—though she is no more and no less responsible than the rest of us. Of course, that isn't the most comforting thought, but it is a sober reminder that this is our fault and not God's. And God did warn us.

The main lesson to learn from this, however, is the enormity of sin and the need to hate it. Shortly after the news of Pat's disease came, I received what seemed to be a rather strange note of condolence from a friend who was teaching at another seminary. After expressing his sorrow over the news, he wrote, "I can just imagine how angry you must be right now at sin." Frankly, I thought that was a rather odd way to console someone. I knew that sin was the last target of my anger, if it was a focus at all.

And yet as I thought about my friend's note, I realized that he was absolutely right. These kinds of tragic events occur because we live in a fallen world. We may think our sins are a trifling matter. But when one hears the diagnosis of a terminal disease, or when one stands at the graveside of a loved one—as we have at my mother's, father's, and brother's graves—one has a vivid illustration of how terrible sin is. God said it would lead to this, but we don't take that warning as seriously as we should until something like this happens.

We may think of sin as trivial, but it isn't. We may also think that the punishment of disease, trouble, and death far outweighs the crime of a little sin. That only underscores how far we are from God's perspective on these things. In light of our relative comfort with sin, a little sin doesn't seem so bad. From the perspective of an absolutely perfect God who has nothing to do with sin, it is atrocious.

Think of it in these terms. If you are a parent, when your children were born, they were totally helpless and depended on you for everything. You nurtured them and provided for their needs. You have loved them deeply, and you express that love in many different ways. In response, all you ask is that your children obey a few simple rules. How do you feel when they disobey? Doesn't it seem like the height of ingratitude to take so much from you and then refuse to follow a few rules? Surely their disobedience seems far more serious to you than to them. How much more must it hurt God, who has given us so much and who moment by moment sustains us in existence, when we disobey him! Viewed from our perspective, sin isn't so bad, but viewing it from God's vantage point, we should see that we need a different perspective on sin altogether.

My friend was right. If we see sin from God's perspective, we need to hate it. When we see where sin ultimately leads, we begin to understand how truly serious it is, and how much we ought to resist it. I can't say this will greatly comfort most of us, but it may help to focus our anger in the right direction. It may also help us to feel more comfortable with God as we realize that ultimately we have brought these things on ourselves. God warned us, but *we* didn't listen. Thank God that now in our troubles *he* will listen, forgive, and restore!

Help Yourself by Helping Others

Other things also helped me cope with our situation. I mentioned earlier that I was having various physical problems and that the stress from my wife's news only made matters worse for me. Within a few months after receiving her diagnosis, I was in great pain and was of little use to anyone. I didn't have the physical stamina to preach or the energy to make it through my classes. I not only felt that our situation was helpless and hopeless, but I also felt that I was useless and that I was adding to the problem by requiring attention that should have been placed elsewhere. As with many people, my feelings of self-worth are tied in large part to my work and productivity. Being barely able to function made my sense of hopelessness worse.

In the midst of this dilemma, the Lord gave me opportunities to help other people. This gave me a chance to shift my focus off our own problems and onto someone else's needs. Even more, it showed me that I could still be useful. Gradually, as I regained strength and was able to do more, I became increasingly thankful that I could do anything, let alone assist others who had shown us so much love and concern.

For those wrestling with some affliction, as you are able, seek ways to help others. There is therapeutic value in getting your eyes off your problems and in seeing again that you can be of use to others. This contributed somewhat to lifting my burdens and showed me that when others, including my family, needed me, through God's enablement I could be of some service to them.

Where Do We Go from Here?

After many months of grieving and after experiencing some healing, I began to ask myself how I would ultimately respond to our problems. I began to consider my options. Would I continue to grieve and fall apart? I had already done that, and it solved nothing. With that approach, there had been little improvement in my own outlook, and I was of little use to anyone else. I concluded that this approach would in no way solve our problems. My wife still needed a husband, my children a father, and my students a teacher; falling apart wouldn't address any of those needs. That option seemed a dead end. As Scripture says, there is a time to mourn (Eccl. 3:4), but then one must get on with life.

Another option was to get on with my life but exclude God from it. Many people choose this option in the face of affliction. They either conclude that there is no God or decide that there is, but they will fight him. Neither was acceptable for me. Though there was still some leftover anger toward God, I had seen too many evidences of his working in my life to doubt his existence. It made no sense to devote my life to propagating the view that God doesn't exist or that he is uninvolved with us. Surely there were more productive things I could do with my life.

Rejecting God's existence was totally unsatisfactory, but choosing to fight him was no better. God's goodness throughout my life—even now in this circumstance—didn't warrant my turning from him. Moreover, it is lunacy to pick a fight you can't win. In addition, it is beyond lunacy to fight someone who, rather than being the cause of your problems, is the only possible answer to them.

Another option was to take a Kierkegaardian leap of faith and trust that somehow this all made sense, though I could explain none of it. In other words, I could simply ignore and bypass the intellect and throw myself on God in the hope that he was there. Some might find that attractive but it wasn't a viable option for me. It is not my nature to sacrifice intellect so completely. The questions and the lack of peace would be there until my mind was settled. I didn't expect to find all the answers, but I knew I had to find many of them.

The only real option for me was clear—to continue trusting and worshiping God and to get on with my life. I had to stop the seemingly interminable deep grieving and allow emotional healing to continue. I had to focus on answers that would satisfy the emotional dimensions of my struggle and would at the same time give enough intellectual answers to warrant peace of mind. I realized that I couldn't wait until all those answers arrived to continue with life, for too many people needed my help, and I needed to give it to them.

As I began to take this approach to my problems (and at some point we all must decide how to respond to our problems), I focused more on the positive things I've already mentioned. The healing and coping process continues to this day, as it will through the rest of my life. Occasionally I wrestle with these issues, but more often I find myself sad and depressed as Pat's disease gets worse and I reflect on how much of her I have lost. It is both amazing and distressing that someone can be physically present, but not really present at all. The presence of her absence continues to be very painful!

Despite such pain, God has allowed me to function again. And another thing that has helped me deal with our situation is the realization that, despite our best wishes and intentions, there are few people who can totally control the circumstances in which they live and minister. Elijah couldn't and neither could Jeremiah, Daniel, or the apostle Paul. When tragedy strikes, one must at some time face a crucial decision—*either* let the tragedy destroy you and then you accomplish little of benefit for anyone, including yourself, *or* choose instead to live for God in spite of the circumstances. That is, play the hand life has dealt you, so to speak, and make the best out of a difficult situation. The apostle Paul is a great example of how to do just that. Put Paul in prison on one occasion, and he converts the jailor to Christ. Put him in prison on another and he writes important letters to growing churches (Ephesians, Philippians, Colossians, Philemon), letters that become part of the New Testament! In a similar way, for me, the second option is the only reasonable choice, and it entails that I keep on trusting God in spite of what is happening.

God Hides the Future So We'll Trust Him

God was not only there when the shock of tragic news first came. At various points along the way when I was ready to hear it, he sent a further word of comfort, encouragement, and enlightenment. One of those words of help comes from what might seem a rather strange source of comfort—a passage in Ecclesiastes. The lesson from it is that God hides the future from us so that we have to trust him. The text says:

Consider what God has done: Who can straighten what he has made crooked? When times are good, be happy; but when times are bad, consider: God has made the one as well as the other. Therefore, a man cannot discover anything about his future. (7:13–14)

The context of these verses is significant. The sixth and seventh chapters of Ecclesiastes contain a series of aphorisms or dictums, although it isn't always easy to see how they fit together. Generally, much of chapter 7 focuses on things that at first appear undesirable in order to show that they do in fact have a certain benefit. Ecclesiastes 6 shows that things that look good at first also have a down side. The ultimate message is that we can't always take things at face value, nor should we think we can always understand them. If this is true of things we do and experience, how much more is it true of God and his ways!

In verses 13–14 (quoted above) the author of Ecclesiastes especially emphasizes the sovereign power of God. Some think the rhetorical question, "Who can straighten what he has made crooked?" means that if God brings something we consider evil, we can't make it good (straighten it). Put another way, we can't overturn God's powerful hand. While this interpretation surely fits verse 14 and its teaching about God's bringing of adversity, I think the writer's point is even more general. That is, just as no one can straighten what God bends, no one can bend what he straightens. No one can overturn what God does, regardless of what it is; man must simply submit to God's providence.

All of this suggests that adversity and prosperity alike are under God's hand. Indeed, the Teacher of Ecclesiastes confirms that in verse 14. God sends both good and bad. He tells us to be happy in the good days. That may seem strange, since most people are inclined to be happy in times of prosperity. However, the injunction to be happy makes an abundant amount of sense. Some people will allow themselves only so much prosperity before they begin to worry about the future. It's as though they are keeping score of how many good things are happening because they believe that we can only have just so much "good luck" before we are due for some really "bad luck." It's as if they think that the more things go well, the more they are "storing up" and postponing some major calamities. Rather than enjoying their present blessings, they worry about how badly they are going to get clobbered once the good times run out. Of course, no one really knows what will come next, so all this worrying about future evil coming our way accomplishes nothing. Just as it is true that things which start out bad can wind up being good, and vice versa, it is also true that when times are good for us, there may be more good times on the docket. But even if what's up next in our lives is suffering, why lose the enjoyment of the present? So, the Teacher tells us to be happy. Don't let the evil that may or may not be just around the corner destroy the happiness of the present.

The writer then says that in evil days, we should "consider." He doesn't say that in evil days we should be sad. He doesn't need to, because that comes naturally. Instead, we should consider. What should we consider or think about? We should think about what has happened, think about the alternation of good and bad, and realize that no one knows when either will come. In fact, what appears to be good may turn out evil, and vice versa. Things aren't always what they seem. But what we should most consider is that God has made both good and bad times, and that he pieces them together in our lives in such a way that we won't know what will happen in the future.

Is this really what the passage says? Indeed it is, for the writer says that God puts together the events of our lives in such a way that "a man cannot discover anything about his future"; that is, God structures our personal histories in a way that conceals the future. Why does God hide the future from us? I wrestled with that question, and there was only one answer that made sense (though it isn't stated in the text). If we don't know what will happen in the future, our only option is to wait on the Lord to reveal what will come next and to trust him about our future. We may want to change what God will do, but verse 13 reminds us that we can't. We must submit to his providence and simply trust him. If we knew the details of our future, we might think we could manipulate and control it without relying on God at all. In short, we might think there was no need to trust God.

God conceals the future, then, so that we must trust him. You can see how this truth fits my family's situation so well. It wasn't only relevant before we learned the news that was for so long available but unknown to us; it has been relevant as we have dealt with the course of this disease and thought about the future of each of our children.

As I thought about this truth, however, I was again troubled. If God conceals the future so that we must trust him, does that mean God manipulates people and events to get us to love and trust him? Is it possible that he can't get our trust any other way, so he arranges things to force us to trust him? If that is so, this is no God worthy of praise and worship! Nor is he a good God! This is a conniving, manipulative God who has created us solely for his benefit and really doesn't care about us after all.

Upon further reflection, however, I realized that God isn't an evil God at all. By concealing the future, God does make us trust him, but this is compassion, not manipulation! It is compassionate in a number of ways.

Knowing the details of our future would probably be harmful to us. Suppose our future would be good. No doubt we would be relieved, but the joy of discovery would be gone. What should be great when it happens would lose its excitement as a surprise. We might even be bored, and the joy of anticipation would be gone. Suppose one year when you were a child you knew exactly what you were getting for Christmas, even though your parents thought you didn't know. Wouldn't that somewhat spoil your joy of discovery on Christmas eve or morning when you opened your presents? Isn't part of the fun of Christmas that until presents are opened, anything seems possible—that we can imagine any number of delightful gifts waiting for us? But if we already know what we're getting, the joy of anticipating something new and unknown is largely removed. Not only that, but if Mom and Dad think you don't know what you're getting, you have to act surprised when you see your presents, even if you've known for a long time what they are. Some of us just aren't good enough actors to pull that off!

Revealing a good future might also make us complacent in our relationship with God, and that would be bad. If we know that the future will be good, we might conclude that we don't need to rely on God, but obviously we do. And we might also very quickly become inattentive to the present and impatient to get to the future as we eagerly await it. This sometimes happens to us even without knowing the specifics of the future. When we anticipate an exciting upcoming vacation, we become impatient with the present. In essence, we overlook the good that is happening now and lose the present. That would be unfortunate, because God may have significant work for us to do now and great blessings in the present as well.

On the other hand, suppose our future will be evil. Unless the Lord returns first for his church, Scripture and common sense teach that the ultimate end of this life for us all will be death, and death is evil. If we knew in advance the circumstances of our death, or if we knew what evils would befall us along the way, we might be totally horrified and unable to act as fear paralyzed us. Hiding the future is compassionate, because if we knew the future it might terrify us.

Hiding an evil future is also compassionate because we must not ignore the present, something we might do if we knew the future. We might spend much of our time worrying about it or grieving over our anticipated misfortune. Even more, we might think that we could somehow change the future to avoid the foreseen evils. Of course, that is impossible, for as the Teacher says, no one can change what God has decided will happen. Why waste the present trying to change something that can't be changed? If we foolishly waste the present, at the end of life we will look back on our life with regrets over never really having lived at all.

As already mentioned, one of the things that our experiences have done for me is to focus my attention more on the present. I don't want to know any more about the distant future than I have to. In fact, I am better able to cope when I focus on where my wife is today, rather than on where she may be in her condition somewhere down the road. We must not become so overly occupied with the future that we lose today. God has hidden the future, so we must just trust him. He is compassionate in doing so.

God's hiding my family's future is also compassionate, because we couldn't handle some of the information about the future if we had it. On November 4, 1987, I caught a glimpse of the future that just about destroyed me. I am more than willing now to take the future one day at a time. In most cases, God compassionately reveals the details of our future moment by moment, and that is enough. As Scripture says, "Each day has enough trouble of its own" (Matt. 6:34). I don't have tomorrow's grace yet, so I don't need to know tomorrow's evil yet either!

GRACE, JUSTICE, AND THE SUFFERING OF THE RIGHTEOUS

Although there were many sources of comfort and encouragement, something was still wrong. There seemed to be a basic unfairness about our situation. Put simply, why was this happening to us, and not also to other people? Wasn't it unjust of God to ask us to bear this burden, especially when others' trials are so much less catastrophic? I believe this is a sticking point for many people that makes it very difficult for them to live with God.

Please do not misunderstand this. I don't wish our pain on anyone, but it seems only fair that if others escape, we should too. Since God has kept others from this fate, why not us as well? Of course, he owes nothing to anyone, but justice seems to demand that we get at least as good a shake as the next family.

I suspect that most people who experience significant tragedy in their lives have such thoughts at some point. I surely had those thoughts, but I came to see that they contain an error. When philosophers discuss the concept of justice, they distinguish between *distributive justice* and *egalitarian justice*. With distributive justice, each person gets exactly what is deserved. If you do good, in strict justice you are owed good. If you do evil, in strict justice you deserve punishment. Egalitarian justice, however, gives everyone the same thing, regardless of merit or desert.

Now I saw the source of the problem. It isn't just that sufferers think distributive justice mandates a better fate for them (since they think they have done good). The complaint is that God should operate with egalitarian justice in his handling of the world. We expect him to treat everyone the same, and that means we should escape a specific affliction if others do! Otherwise, it seems that God has been unfair.

Once I remembered the distinction between these two types of justice, I immediately asked why God is obligated to dole out suffering and blessing on the basis of egalitarian justice. Given the demands of distributive justice, all sinners *deserve* nothing but punishment. Why, then, is God obligated to respond to us in egalitarian terms? I couldn't answer that. If God really did handle us according to egalitarian justice, we would all either experience the same torture or be equally blessed. But those ideas don't match the God described in Scripture. It was a tremendous help to realize that part of my anger stemmed from thinking that God is obligated to handle us with egalitarian justice. Once I realized that he has no such obligation, I understood that much of my anger rested on a misunderstanding of what God should be expected to do.

Now this didn't completely solve the problem. Even if God isn't obligated to give any of us more than we deserve, and even if we deserve punishment for our sin, still God has chosen to be *gracious* to some. If you are suffering from some affliction, you may feel that God should extend the same grace to you as he has to those who never have to deal with an affliction that is anywhere near as horrible as yours. So it seems that God must be unjust for not extending as much grace to you as to the next person.

This objection makes a lot of sense, and I believe it was at the heart of what was then bothering me. Nonetheless, it is still wrong. The complaint against God has now escalated from a demand that God treat us with egalitarian *justice* to a demand that God grant us egalitarian *grace*.

But this is wrong in at least two respects. First, God is no more obligated to give the same *grace* to everyone than he is to give egalitarian *justice* to all. He is only obligated to distribute what we deserve. The other point is that since we are talking about granting grace, the charge that God has been *unjust* because he gave someone else more *grace* (and this is really what the sufferer is complaining about) is totally misguided.

Grace is unmerited favor, and that means that you get something good that you don't deserve and didn't earn. If God *owes* no one any grace at all (if he owed it, it wouldn't be grace, but justice), then it can't be *unjust* for others to get more grace than I get. It can only be unjust if God is obligated to treat us with egalitarian grace, and he surely isn't. In fact, he isn't *obligated* to treat us with any kind of grace. Grace precludes obligation! That's why it's grace and not justice. Hence, it can't be unjust if someone gets more grace than another. If God graciously chooses to give some people a better lot in life than others, he has done nothing wrong. We have no right to place requirements on how and when God distributes grace; if we did, that would turn it into justice.

This distinction between grace and justice is crucial. Many people seem to think that grace is the opposite of injustice. Hence, when God doesn't give them grace, they conclude that God has treated them unfairly. But the opposite of injustice is justice; grace is an entirely different thing. Put differently, grace is neither fair nor unfair, because fairness and unfairness invoke the concept of justice. Grace has nothing to do with justice; it's a different commodity altogether!

One of Jesus's parables vividly illustrates the point about the relation of grace to justice. It is the parable of the landowner and the workers in his vineyard, recorded in Matthew 20:1–16. In many respects this is a strange and difficult parable, but its message about the relation of grace to justice is extremely important. It teaches that God has the right to give grace as he chooses, and when he does, no one has the right to envy those who receive God's unmerited favor or to complain that God has treated him or her unfairly because he gave them less grace than others received or didn't give them grace at all.

Jesus begins this parable by saying that it illustrates how he handles things in the kingdom of heaven (v. 1). Jesus says that a landowner went out early in the morning to hire workers for his vineyard. In order to understand the story more fully, it is important to know that the Jews divided the day from sunrise to sunset into twelve parts. Thus, the sixth hour would be noon, the third would be 9 a.m., the ninth hour would be 3 p.m., and the eleventh hour would be 5 p.m., just a little while before quitting time. The landowner agreed to pay those hired first in the day a denarius for a whole day of work, and he sent them off to work (v. 2). According to verses 3–5, he hired more workers at 9 a.m., noon, and 3 p.m. (the third, sixth, and ninth hours). In each instance, he told them to go into the vineyard and work, and he promised that he would give them whatever is right. He didn't say how much money would be "right," but in essence he promised to do what was fair. About an hour before quitting time, he saw some other workers who hadn't worked at all that day, and he sent them out to work too (vv. 6–7). So only in the case of the workers hired first did the landowner promise a specific wage. All the remaining workers agreed to trust that the landowner would do right by them.

At the end of the day, the landowner told his steward to call in all the workers and pay them. He stipulated, however, that the steward should first pay those hired last and work his way back to those hired first. Only by crafting the parable in this way do we get to hear the response of the workers hired first, and only after giving their response can Jesus make the point of his parable.

What did the landowner pay those hired later in the day? Justice would seem to dictate that he pay them less than what he paid those hired early in the day. But he didn't. He paid the workers hired last a denarius (v. 9). In fact, he gave each of the laborers hired throughout the day a denarius. When those hired first saw that those hired last received a denarius, they must have been metaphorically licking their chops, expecting a bonanza. After all, if those who did next to nothing got a denarius, those who worked the whole day should get more, or so they reasoned. But the steward paid to each of those hired first in the day exactly what he paid to everyone else, a denarius (v. 10).

The workers hired first were furious! They had done most of the work. They had labored through the heat of the day, and yet they received no more pay than those hired just about an hour before quitting time. That seemed totally unfair to them and they complained to the landowner about what he had done. Surely they should have received more than these other workers.

What these workers did is so typical of human nature. Somebody got a better deal in life than we did, and that's not fair. We can't stand it when others prosper and we don't, especially if we think we are just as good as they are or that we have worked just as hard or harder than they. We complain that if there were any justice in the world, we would succeed and be blessed at least as much as others.

Verses 13–15 record the landowner's response. The landowner replied that he had done nothing wrong in his treatment of the workers hired first. Didn't he agree to pay them a denarius for a day's work? Of course he did (v. 2)! They did the work, and he paid them. Justice says that you pay exactly what you owe. The landowner made a deal with the workers. They kept their part of the bargain, and so did he. He gave them exactly what he promised; they had no reason to be angry, for he had treated them fairly.

In verse 15 we read that the landowner then asked them a crucial question: "Don't I have the right to do what I want with my own money?" If he wanted to pay those hired later in the day exactly what he paid those hired first, didn't he have a right to do that? Was the problem here that the workers hired first were envious of those who seemed to get a better deal than they did (v. 15)? Indeed, it was; the landowner had been generous (gracious) to these other workers. The workers hired first were in effect demanding that the landowner treat everyone with justice—that is, give each exactly what he had earned, merited, deserved. Nothing less and certainly nothing more. Or perhaps they were implicitly claiming that since the landowner had been generous to the other workers (extended them grace), he *owed* it to *them* to be gracious and generous as well.

But this last sentence is confusing. Think again about the promise the landowner made to all the laborers except those hired first. He told them that he would give them whatever was right, but he never stipulated a specific monetary amount. So his only obligation was to do something right (just) for them. Was giving them each a denarius treating them justly or rightly? Yes and no. Yes, because if those who worked less than the whole day received the same as those hired first in the day, the landowner certainly hadn't been unjust to those who worked a shorter time. He had done for them what anyone certainly should call right.

On the other hand, he wasn't just to those hired later in the day, but not because he was unjust to them! As it turned out, he decided to be more than just—he decided to be gracious. In light of what he paid those hired first, he gave the rest of the workers more than they deserved! Had he done something wrong to any of the workers? Of course not. Whatever was owed, he paid, but out of the goodness of his heart in some cases he gave well beyond anything that was owed. It is all right not to give exactly what is owed as long as you don't give *less* than is owed. The landowner gave most of the workers more than he owed. That's not justice but it's not injustice either. It's grace! What is so wrong with giving some people exactly what they deserve (justice) while granting to others more than they deserve (grace)? After all, didn't the landowner have a right to do with his money what he wanted? Whose money (grace) was it, anyway?

So, then, the landowner was fair (just) to those hired first, because he gave them exactly what he had promised and they had earned. But, still, isn't there a sense in which the landowner still *owed* them more, since he gave the workers hired later more than they deserved? Absolutely not, and this is the crucial point. He didn't owe them more, because *grace* is *never* owed! You see, grace and justice are two totally different things. The workers hired first in the day were envious of the grace given to the other workers. Jesus's point was that they had no reason to be angry at the landowner or to envy their coworkers. How small of them to begrudge these others the grace they received, and to think the landowner was unfair because he *owed* them more. Grace is never *owed* to anyone, so God cannot rightly be accused of failing to do something he should have done when someone else receives grace that we didn't get!

Jesus ends this parable by affirming that it shows that the last shall be first and the first shall be last. What did Jesus mean? We must understand this within the context of the discussion between Jesus and his disciples, recorded at the end of chapter 19 (vv. 16–30). Jesus had just told a rich young man the cost of discipleship. It involves selling his earthly possessions, giving to the poor, and then following Christ. The disciples were very much disturbed by this saying. Peter told the Lord that he and the others had left everything to follow Christ; what would God do for them? Jesus replied that those who leave earthly possessions and family will be given a position of prominence in the kingdom when Christ reigns. They can't sacrifice more than God will bless them. However, Jesus reminded them that many who are last will be first, and the first will be last.

Amidst this context, Jesus then tells the parable of the landowner and the laborers in his vineyard. At its end (20:16), Jesus repeats the point that the last will be first and the first will be last. This sounds strange, but within the context of the parable, I believe it makes an abundant amount of sense. If our position in the kingdom is based on things like our earthly possessions, fame, and accomplishments, then those with the most impressive résumés would have the greatest authority in the kingdom. On the other hand, if God bases privilege and position in the kingdom on the magnanimity of his grace, then our accomplishments aren't so important, and even someone who in this life is last (socially, economically, etc.) could be placed in a position of prominence. If a loving heavenly Father wants to extend them such grace, the rest of us have no right to be offended or complain!

I believe that these great truths apply to my situation and to every instance where someone feels that God has treated them unfairly because they don't receive exemption from problems that others escape. God isn't obligated to keep me from my trials just because he hasn't given you those afflictions. Giving grace to you doesn't mean he has been unfair to me. He never obligated himself to give me such grace, so there is no injustice in what he has done (or not done). I have no right to think he has been unjust or unfair to me by withholding grace, for being unfair would mean he failed to give me grace that he owed me, but grace (*un*merited favor) is *never owed* to anyone. And I have no right to envy you when God gives you grace he has withheld from me, because he has a right to do with his own grace whatever he chooses.

Rather than envying the grace others receive, I should be thankful that they received grace. Surely I would not be happy to see God withhold grace so that others are struck with the same tragedy that has befallen us. Moreover, we must all be careful not to assume that because God has withheld *a particular* grace from us that he has withheld *all* grace. There are too many examples in my life of God's unmerited favor for me ever to think that. Not least among those undeserved blessings are the wonderful wife and children he has given me.

These principles about justice and grace won't likely relieve the pain of suffering, but they can help dissipate anger toward God. I have found them to be liberating, and I frequently remind myself of these principles when I am inclined to lament that God has given others an apparently easier lot than mine.

There is another lesson for all of us to learn from these points about the relation of grace to justice. Suppose that you, not others, are the one who receives God's gracious exemption from suffering. Don't reject those who suffer as morally and spiritually inferior to you just because you received grace! You didn't get that grace because you are better—if you had, it would be a reward for your accomplishments. And that wouldn't be grace; that would be justice. No one should feel superior for having received grace, because they did nothing to earn it—that's why it's grace.

So when others don't get the same grace you do, should you feel guilty that they got affliction while you received grace? These questions are not just theoretical; they are relevant to my family's situation. Earlier I mentioned the dilemma about whether to have our children tested for Huntington's disease. Obviously there are problems for those found to carry the gene, but there is also a difficulty for those who learn they won't get the disease. It is not uncommon for those who test negative for the disease to feel guilty that they will escape while their brothers or sisters won't.

Viewed in the light of what I have been saying, I believe that no one should feel guilty for escaping affliction. If what happens is totally a matter of justice—that is, if we all get exactly what we deserve—then I should feel guilty if you suffer and I don't. But this isn't a matter of simple justice. It is a matter of grace. If God in his sovereign wisdom chooses to give you grace, don't feel guilty as though either you or God has done something wrong. Rather, rejoice and praise him for the grace that spared you the suffering.

In addition, feel compassion toward those who haven't escaped, and do whatever you can to help them bear their burdens.

If you are the recipient of affliction, never begrudge others the grace God gave them. If you receive God's gracious exemption from suffering, praise him and show compassion to those who suffer. Don't apologize for receiving grace, and don't seek affliction in an attempt to "even things out" between you and those who are suffering. Affliction will find its way to your doorstep soon enough. Praise God for the grace!

These principles about grace and justice also apply to many other areas of our lives. Let me just mention two that relate to salvation. Sometimes critics of Christianity complain that our God is said to have power to save anyone he wants from sin. In fact, he could save us all if he wanted to. But he is said to have chosen only to save some, leaving the rest for eternal damnation. How can it be fair to save only some when, as Christians claim, no one merits salvation?

You don't have to believe in divine election to know that God doesn't save everyone. But are the critics right? Has God been unfair in his handling of salvation? If these questions are meant to assert that God should handle the granting of salvation with fairness, then they invoke the concept of justice. But if justice is the requirement, then all of us are in deep trouble. Scripture and common sense tell us that all have sinned and are guilty before God. If God decided to treat everyone with strict justice, no one would be saved. However, a gracious God has decided to save some people for a life of eternal fellowship with him and for abundant life now; no one who is saved merits salvation.

Some will undoubtedly complain that others are no more or less deserving, but they aren't saved. This is true, but if we demand that God treat us according to what we deserve, then those not saved receive their just due. To complain that God owes these people salvation since he has graciously granted it to others is to place obligations on grace. But grace cannot be obligated; it is a free gift bestowed out of the generous heart of the giver. Those who don't get saving grace have nothing to complain about, for God hasn't failed to do something he owed them.

These principles about the relation of grace to justice also apply to another item relating to God's handling of salvation. Some of us decided early in life to give up much of what the world counts as pleasure in order to trust Christ as Savior and live for him. We did so not because we wouldn't have enjoyed any of those pleasures but because we were told that Christians just don't do such things. On the other hand, others accept Christ late in life, some even while in the throes of a terminal illness. Some may have turned to Christ only after having indulged in all of the pleasures and even evils this world has to offer. Think of the thief crucified next to Christ. As he was dying, he placed his faith and trust in Christ. Christ told him that he would be with Christ in paradise that very same day.

Readers who have known Christ as personal Savior for much of your life, I have a question for you. When you get to heaven, are you going to say something like the following to the Lord: "Lord, I'm just so thrilled to be here! Thank you so much for saving me! But, Lord, something is bothering me. That repentant thief who was crucified next to you—I don't know what he did in his life, but at least he did something bad enough to get himself crucified. On the other hand, there are many things I would have enjoyed doing, but I didn't so that I could faithfully follow you. Are you going to tell me, Lord, that I am no more saved than that repentant thief who turned to you only in the last minutes of his life? That's not fair, Lord! For the first five hundred thousand years or so of eternity you should leave him outside the walls of heaven (no, don't cast him into hell; after all, he did trust you as Savior). And then when you do bring him inside heaven's gates, don't give him one of those bright shiny mansions on Main Street. Put him far from sight—a back alley or even someone's garage would be appropriate for him."

When you get to heaven, are you going tell the Lord *that*? Of course not! You won't be unhappy that others received eternal life after a life of indulgence in sin, while you chose to live a life of obedience to God. Would you prefer that God not extend them grace so that they would spend eternity separated from God— just because they trusted Christ late in life? Of course not! Never begrudge someone the grace God gives him or her. I am delighted that our God is so gracious and patient with sinners that he leaves the door to salvation open even for those who repeatedly reject him before they turn to him as Savior. There is no room for envying the grace God gives to others!

Even those who don't know Christ as Savior have still received grace from his hand. Otherwise they would have received judgment long ago, as would those who know Christ. And even though my family and I didn't receive grace that exempts us from Huntington's disease, we are still the recipients of his grace in many areas. These truths about grace and justice don't turn evil things that happen into good, but in my case, understanding them did remove a huge obstacle to fellowship between the Lord and me. He hasn't failed to give me any good thing he owed! And I must add that he has granted many gracious blessings to me and my family that he didn't owe. Grace is not fair, but it isn't unfair either! It is something entirely different, and I thank God for it!

DECEIVED BY GOD?

In previous chapters I have shared various lessons I have learned through our life experiences, and things that helped me to cope with our situation. But there were still a couple of issues raised along the way that bothered me. I knew that until I resolved them, they would continue to gnaw at me. I begin with the question of whether you could seek and find God's will only to wind up in a situation with severe affliction, something you expressly asked God to keep you from. And this raises the interesting theological question of whether on some occasions God gets us to do his will by withholding information from us, information that would have kept us from the situation. But this is more than just a question of purely intellectual interest. It is a question about the kind of God we have and serve.

For a long time, one of the most troubling aspects of our situation was how it all came about. I know that no mere human can completely control the course of his or her life. But it seems that most people at least get to choose to make the most of their circumstances or to try to rise above their life situation, if it is difficult. This is especially so if you make choices you believe God has called you to make. The circumstances I have described are surely not the life and ministry I would have chosen. As I have shared, it appeared I did have a choice about these things, for I didn't have to go into ministry, and I didn't have to marry Pat. Once we married, we didn't have to have children. Pat and I did make those decisions. But once we got Pat's diagnosis, it seemed that I had made those choices under false pretenses. I believed God was leading me to choose one sort of life, when in fact I wound up with exactly the life I was trying to avoid. In fact, I was saddled with a situation worse than anything I could have ever dreamed in my worst nightmare.

For a long time I was hurt and anguished by the thought that somehow God deceived me into marrying Pat by hiding information that could have saved me from my present circumstances. There were also questions about knowing and doing God's will. Was it really not God's will that I marry Pat and that we have children? Could I have been that mistaken about God's design for my life? Or was it really God's will that I marry her, but when one follows the Lord's leading one can expect to be double-crossed? How can one teach theology and write books about God, and yet be apparently so mistaken about how God works in people's lives?

Such thoughts are among the most disturbing that I faced over the years, and they have been as disruptive to my relationship with the Lord as anything that I have ever experienced. I was raised in a home where a high premium was placed on telling the truth. If our word can't be trusted, what are we really worth? This is part of the very core of my outlook on and approach to life. How utterly distressing, then, when God, the very embodiment of truth, appeared to have deceived me!

Clearly, I needed to sort all of this out. After some years of wrestling with these questions, and after most of my feelings of anger toward God were gone, I came to terms with what God had done and how he had done it.

Was I deceived by God? I believe that I was in fact deceived, but not by God. Though it is hard to accept blame for such a critical error as this, I see now that I deceived myself. Given my background and the circumstances surrounding my meeting and marrying Pat, I constructed a case for a life relatively free of troubles. But that wasn't the only possible conclusion to infer from God's leading me to marry Pat and start a family. Let me explain.

My mother's illnesses and the strain they placed upon my father and his ministry made me conclude that anyone embarking on such a ministry would be best able to fulfill that work with a healthy wife and children. I knew that God was calling me to a life of scholarship, preaching, and teaching. I reasoned that whomever God would have me marry would be healthy, or at least not so unhealthy as to jeopardize the ministry God was giving me. All of this seemed logical and reasonable enough.

I approached dating and marriage armed with that mind-set, which was natural. Someone raised in the home of an alcoholic, for example, would likely be very careful not to marry an alcoholic. I knew it would not be impossible to minister effectively if I had a wife whose health was poor, because I had seen my father do it. But it would be easier to minister without such a hindrance. God knew that, and so did I. I concluded, then, that if I was careful about such matters, God would probably not lead me to marry someone whose health would stand in the way of the work he had given me to do.

When Pat came into my life and we began to get serious about one another, we were very concerned about disobeying God's will. It was not the matter of her health that troubled us at that point, but rather the apparently incompatible forms of ministry to which we thought God was calling us. God resolved that issue, however, in a way that neither of us originally expected, showing us that we could minister together without contradicting his will for our lives in the slightest. The only other question concerned Pat's health, but it was exceptionally good at that time. There were no signs of what was to come, and we were assured that what had happened to her mother wouldn't be passed to Pat.

My love for Pat, my belief about the need to have a healthy wife, my assurance that Pat wouldn't get her mother's disease, and the clear leading of the Lord concerning our respective ministries led me to conclude that God wanted us together. Though such thinking is sound, it is still an example of inferential reasoning.

Inferential reasoning is reasoning from facts that are clearly known to a conclusion that is not known but seems necessitated by the facts we do know. For example, Scripture clearly teaches that there is only one God. Just as clearly, however, it refers to three distinct persons (Father, Son, and Holy Spirit) as God. From such clear biblical truths, Christians throughout church history have concluded that the right way to think of God is as triune. Nowhere in Scripture do we find the word *Trinity*, nor does any passage say "God is one as to his essence or nature but three as to the manifestations of that nature." Nonetheless, such a doctrinal conclusion seems inevitable on the basis of what Scripture clearly teaches about God.

Although the inference to the doctrine of the Trinity is a natural and accurate inference, and although evangelicals affirm that Holy Scripture does teach this doctrine, even so, inferential reasoning is notoriously risky. For example, a skeptic might look at the biblical data we raise in support of the Trinity and disagree with our conclusion. He might say that the data present three gods instead of one. And he might infer that passages about one God mean that the three gods normally agree and work together. Or he might suggest that the writers who say there is only one God are simply wrong.

Though we would say the skeptic has drawn an incorrect inference from the data, we would be wrong if we said the skeptic's inferences were impossible conclusions to make. From precisely the same information, it may be possible to draw several conclusions.

Consider another example. From the fossil records the atheistic scientist concludes that evolution is correct; but from the same data, a Christian scientist finds scientific support and evidence for a Creator. How can this be since the "facts" are the same for both the Christian and the non-Christian? This shows just how tricky inferential reasoning can be.

So it was in my case. From my reasoning about needing a healthy family in order to be free to minister, from the information we had at that time about Pat's health and the health of her family, from the Lord's leading regarding our respective ministries, and from the love he placed within us for each other, it was thoroughly logical to infer that we should marry and that health wouldn't curtail us. What I came to see some years ago is that while such inferences were natural ones to make and could have been correct, they weren't the only ones that were possible from the data we had. The conclusions I reached were reasonable, and they surely matched what I wanted to happen. But our best-case scenarios don't always match what God has planned for us, even when we think we can build a rational case that things are going to turn out just the way we want.

So where was the mistake in my thinking? Had God actually deceived me? Or had I mistakenly drawn the wrong inference from the information I had? I was certainly not wrong about my love for Pat, or hers for me. Nor was I mistaken that God wanted us to marry and minister together. I didn't have all the information I now know about Pat's health, but is God to blame for that? He could only be blamed for not giving me the pertinent information if he was *obligated* to give it to me before we married.

Yet what could possibly place God under such an obligation as that? For a long time I thought that the need for my wife to be healthy in order for me to accomplish my ministry was enough to obligate God to inform me somehow about the potential health risks of a prospective mate. That belief made me infer from the facts as I knew them at the time not only that I was to marry Pat, but also that she wouldn't have any major ongoing health concerns.

In believing all of these things, I deceived myself into thinking I was getting a different life than I have. Having called me to the ministry and having led me to Pat, God was only obligated to inform me of her medical history before we married if it would be impossible to carry on his work with a wife in poor health. In fact, it is not. From my dad's case, I knew that it is easier for someone in ministry to have a healthy family. I also knew from his case that it is *possible* to minister very effectively even if your wife or other family members are in poor health. Moreover, I came to see that God's intended service for Pat and me is a bit different than we anticipated, and it is service we can do on behalf of the kingdom even though she has this serious illness.

The truth is that God had never promised me anything about my wife's health. I simply saw what I thought would be preferable for someone like myself, and I wrongly concluded that God would do it. It made logical sense, but it wasn't accurate.

Yes, I was deceived, but not by God. He didn't tell me anything that was false, nor did he mislead me. He wasn't obligated to inform me before we married that Pat was even at risk for Huntington's disease, let alone that she would get it.

I have written much about being deceived by God. I have done so for several reasons. For one thing, it is such an important part of my own story. Beyond that, getting this question settled has been a major factor in fully restoring a positive attitude toward God. Sorting out this issue solved a key intellectual problem, a problem that had heightened my emotional and spiritual pain. What has happened and continues to happen to Pat hurts very deeply, but at least my frustration and anger over the situation are no longer directed toward God. Believe me, there is a very uneasy feeling that comes with being angry at the only person who can solve your problem. Thank God, that uneasy feeling and that anger are gone!

I have also shared this at length, hoping it will help my readers. Though no one's circumstances are exactly identical to mine, everyone needs to be reminded how easy it is to build an incorrect case against God through inferential reasoning. Before looking at circumstances and inferring that God has deceived you or done anything else wrong, remember that the conclusion you are drawing may not be the only one possible. It is more likely that you are reading the evidence the wrong way. Before you accuse God over what you think he has done or failed to do, look again at the evidence and be sure that you have interpreted it correctly. Be sure that what you have inferred is the only and the most likely correct thing to conclude. If you look long enough and hard enough, I firmly believe you will see that God isn't guilty of any wrongdoing, and that it is possible to read the evidence in such a way that it in no way implicates God in any deception or other evil.

What about the other question posed in chapter 1 of this book? Could one seek, find, and do God's will and get affliction in response? If by this we are asking whether God would respond to our obedience by sending affliction as a punishment, the answer is an obvious no. God doesn't send suffering as a punishment for doing his will. The Bible amply underscores that the one who obeys God will only receive blessing from God's hand in response to that obedience. The God of the Scriptures isn't an evil fiend who rewards us for obeying him by punishing us with pain and suffering.

On the other hand, there is more to the question than just this. While God won't *punish* us with affliction for obeying his will, doing God's will doesn't guarantee that there will be no affliction when we obey. This sounds paradoxical, but it isn't. God won't send affliction in *punishment* for our obedience, but if we are faithful to God's plan, Satan won't be pleased. The adversary often takes out his displeasure by afflicting the people of God. The truth is that the more we are in the center of God's will, the more we are capturing ground against the enemy of God. Hence, the more we obey God's will, the more we can expect Satan's attacks on us in an effort to discourage and dissuade us from accomplishing God's purposes.

Yes, there will sometimes be affliction when we do God's will, but it doesn't come as punishment from God's hand. This is part of living in a fallen world. And Scripture is also very clear that those who follow God are engaged in a war with those who don't (Eph. 6:12; 1 Peter 5:8–9). Satan will do his best to attack us and to use bad things that happen in a sinful world to destroy us and our faith. Thankfully, the book of Job shows that there is nothing Satan can do that the Almighty doesn't know, permit, and control. We are engaged in a spiritual war. Do we think we can go to war, even be in the front lines of the battle, and never be wounded?

I think many Christians naïvely think just that—if they think about spiritual warfare at all. I certainly never expected a wound quite like the one we got. I have come to see, however, that this expectation was unrealistic. The enemy is very real and has many ways of attacking those who would follow the Lord. There was no way of knowing in advance that we would get an attack of the sort we did, but that just illustrates how crafty and unfair Satan is in the way he uses tragedies to undermine the faith of God's people! Expect him to do the *expected and the unexpected*. Knowing there will be battle wounds doesn't mean the wounds don't hurt, but it can help us assess more accurately what has happened. One may wish exemption from the battle, but that isn't possible. One may even think of changing sides, as many do when confronted with tragedy, but that option isn't the answer to our problems for either time or eternity. And certainly, it is far worse to arouse God's anger than to evoke Satan's!

LIVING WITH DYING

In previous chapters I have told the story of what happened to my wife and what I learned from it in the years after she was first diagnosed. But it is now more than twenty-eight years since we first learned that she has Huntington's. That's a long time to live with someone who is slowly dying—even longer when that someone is the love of your life and there is nothing you can do to stop what is happening to her! The same old feelings of helplessness and hopelessness are always there, but increasingly they are joined with a growing loneliness as the Pat I married slips slowly and irreversibly away.

I wish I could write that the things shared in previous chapters give me all the comfort and strength I need to go on. To a certain extent they do, for at the very least what I have learned from the Lord in dealing with what is happening still answers many of the basic questions I had when Pat was first diagnosed. Those issues don't overwhelm me like they used to, but as I see her disease take its toll, the pain of intellectual and spiritual doubts is increasingly replaced by sadness and loneliness over the person I am gradually losing. Of course, I cannot simply sit back and reflect on what is happening and feel sorry for her or myself. For her deteriorating condition means that there are always new challenges, new difficult decisions, and new disappointments as we watch this disease take from me such a special person. In this chapter I want to share some of the most significant things that have happened over the last decade and a half.

From Partner to Patient

Pat and I have now been married for more than forty-three years. It has been a wonderful experience, because there could not be a better match for me! Very early in our marriage, I would ask Pat's opinion on issues we were facing. I did this because a husband should consult his wife and consider her wishes and counsel. Of course, I often had decided what I wanted to do before asking her opinion, but still I knew it was only right to ask what she thought. It only took a few times, however, for me to see that this woman I married has incredibly uncommon common sense. Most of the time we agreed on what we should do, but I could talk for ten to fifteen minutes, setting forth the pros and cons of an issue and explaining which I thought were stronger. I would then turn to Pat and ask what she thought. Amazingly, time after time, in one or two sentences Pat would say something that made more sense than all the verbiage I had produced in presenting the case for each option. This was so even when we agreed on what we should do. On those rare occasions when we disagreed, I always found her counsel extremely helpful and, more often than not, she was right.

I share all of this because it is but one illustration of how much and how quickly in our marriage I saw her as my partner. Of course, she was everything (and more) that I had hoped for in a wife, but her wisdom, judgment, and ability to see things in helpful ways that I hadn't recognized made her a trusted adviser. I found myself consulting her on all sorts of decisions (big and small), knowing that I was getting advise that was incredibly sensible, and knowing that it was coming from someone whose thoughts were motivated entirely by her love for me.

By the time we reached the year 2000, however, there were significant changes in Pat's condition. Up to that time the most noticeable symptoms had been physical. Occasionally, Pat might fail to remember something that had happened, but that was rare. Between 2000 and 2004 major physical changes happened. Increasingly, it became difficult for Pat to walk, and so more and more we had to rely on a wheelchair. Several years prior to this, we had installed a chair lift in our house that went from the main floor to the upper floor. Early on Pat rarely needed to use the chair lift to maneuver the stairs. But little by little her condition made it clear that she could not safely climb the stairs. Without the chair lift, Pat probably would have lost her balance on the stairs many times.

By 2004 three other major changes occurred, all of them results of the disease taking its toll on her physical abilities. It was for a long time becoming harder for Pat to swallow and to eat normal food. By 2001 a feeding tube was needed. As I now write this, it has been about a decade since we have even tried to give her any food by mouth, for fear that she might choke on something or that she might aspirate liquid that would go into her lungs. Within the following year, it became necessary for Pat to use a full-time catheter, and by the end of 2003 an operation was performed to give her an ileostomy as her body could no longer eliminate waste properly.

At that time, she could still talk and understood most of what she heard in conversations. It was, however, becoming increasingly difficult for her to process mentally what was being said. And at times when I would ask her advice or wonder about her wishes, she was able to articulate very helpfully what she was thinking. But I saw those abilities, too, gradually diminish.

I didn't want to admit it or face it, but I feared that Pat's needs would require expertise that was beyond my physical abilities to provide. Meanwhile, I was determined to keep Pat at home as long as possible and to care for her myself. And for many years that worked, even as it became physically challenging to meet the demands posed by her diminishing abilities. Amazingly, the Lord allowed us to continue to vacation and travel together long distances (including trips out of the country) for the purpose of ministry.

As hard as the physical demands were, emotionally the most difficult thing was that Pat's mental abilities had decreased to a point where we could no longer have conversations about anything like we had before. Though I wanted desperately to keep Pat in the home and care for her, by the end of 2005 the time to move her to a nursing home was drawing near.

Let me affirm emphatically that it is a terrible thing when your life's partner becomes your patient! I am not referring to all the work this involves for the caregiver; indeed, that is a challenge, and in our case there was little or no help with the demands of Pat's care. The hardest thing is when your partner, the love of your life, with whom you've shared everything and with whom you've built a life and home, can no longer *function* as your partner. I am not a physician, nor do I have any formal medical training, but my wife became my patient anyway. Doctors could give advice and prescribe whatever medications might address Pat's various symptoms, but the caregiving fell on me. And unlike every other challenge we faced during our marriage, this time Pat could not help me either with advice or with carrying out the actions that her condition demanded.

Sadly, by this time, our children were living far from us, and because so much time had passed since the initial shock of Pat's disease had come, friends just weren't thinking about us other than to offer an occasional prayer. I think that in general, Christians are willing to engage in concerted prayer and offer tangible help when tragedy first strikes. But as time passes and those afflicted seem to be coping with the situation, friends tend to forget about the ongoing needs. I think this is human nature, and I know that I fall into the same patterns of behavior when others suffer and time moves months and years beyond the initial crises.

Although I was overwhelmed by the increasing physical demands on me in caring for Pat, I was emotionally not ready for what was becoming increasingly clear about the next step in her care. I began to search for ways to get help caring for Pat in the home. The cost of in-home care is not cheap, but it is much less expensive than paying for care in a nursing home. Unfortunately, I quickly learned that though one can hire caregivers to come to one's home, no insurance company will pay for those services.

As it became clear that Pat would need to be in a nursing home, the Lord had provided several key resources. Back in 1995, when our sons were still living at home and Pat's abilities were starting to dwindle significantly, a rather frightening thought had pressed itself upon me: what if I were to die or become incapacitated; how could Pat on her own care for herself and our sons? I could see no way that she would be able to manage such a situation. It was clearly time to think about estate planning. The Lord led us at that time to a very fine lawyer. I explained our situation and asked if there was any legal way to guard my family and our estate from depletion by my wife's disease. I wasn't optimistic that there would be a favorable answer. But much to my surprise and amazement, the lawyer explained that there are federal and state laws that allow people to get assistance in dealing with catastrophic disease. These laws do not require a patient's family to invest all of its assets in the care of their loved one. The lawyer explained what needed to be done, and he drew up the legal documents to do it.

Needless to say, that first visit to the lawyer was quite a shock—a very good one. But what would happen if Pat ever had to go into a nursing home? Would all the legal steps we had taken be overturned? Would the strategy outlined in 1995 really work? By 2007 it was clearly time to find out, because I could no longer meet the physical demands of caring for Pat alone. I returned to the lawyer we used in 1995. I was dismayed when he told me that he set up estates to deal with catastrophic disease, but he had never filed an application for any patient to get assistance from the government in helping to pay for a nursing home.

Thankfully, in my church there is a man who at one time owned and ran a nursing home in northern Illinois. I asked him what to do. He was familiar with the laws involved, and he also had first-hand knowledge of nursing homes in the metropolitan Chicago area. Through his advice (and that of another lawyer), we were led to a lawyer whose practice specializes in elder law. I made an appointment to see her, and within the first minutes of the meeting I knew I'd come to the right person. She had filed many applications for Medicaid, and she knew all the ins and outs of how to do this.

Eventually, we found a nursing home for Pat. Visiting many different ones in northeastern Illinois was quite eye-opening; I can certainly affirm that not all nursing homes are created equal. In the midst of the emotional turmoil of this already difficult decision, where I was acknowledging that my loved one's condition had gotten so bad that I needed professional help to care for her, I was also faced with the financial stress of figuring out how to work the Medicaid system which didn't allow Pat to apply for assistance prior to being a resident in a nursing home.

When Pat moved into a nursing home, I had to pay a deposit of one month's fees, plus the amount it would cost for the first month of care. This amounted to around $13,000—indeed, nursing homes are not cheap, and this was back in November 2007. I didn't have that kind of money in my checking account, so I paid for it with credit cards. But the Lord had a very welcome surprise in store for us.

My lawyer had been preparing the Medicaid application all summer, and filed it once Pat moved into the nursing home on November 15. Early in December, I received a call from a nurse at the nursing home. She asked about the brand of liquid food Pat used, because it was time to order a new batch. She wanted to know so that she could place the order and bill Medicaid. I told her that we had applied for Medicaid but hadn't yet heard whether Pat had been approved for it. The nurse told me that she saw in her computer that Pat was a Medicaid patient. After a few calls to government health agencies, I confirmed that Pat had been approved for Medicaid.

Needless to say, we were overwhelmed when we learned that within fourteen days after our lawyer submitted the Medicaid application, it was approved. And the approval was retroactive to the day she moved into the facility! All of the money I had given the nursing home would be refunded. I found this very hard to believe—government agencies never move that quickly! Clearly, God's hand was in all of this. We again had a vivid reminder of the goodness of the Lord.

Living Together Separately

When we moved Pat into a nursing home, there were many more lessons yet to be learned. The first ones were about nursing homes. I naïvely had thought that once Pat was in a nursing home, she would be cared for properly. After all, she would be under the supervision of many capable caregivers. All of them were much younger than I and all of them were health care professionals. Very quickly I was rudely awakened to some basic facts.

First, things don't always go right even in a nursing home. Pat had good caregivers, so competence wasn't the issue. But I immediately saw that there were far more patients than caregivers. If several patients needed immediate attention, there just weren't enough caregivers to handle all of them. In addition, I had been emptying Pat's catheter and ostomy bags for years, so I presumed that professionals would be well versed in doing the same. Some were, but many had never had a patient with Pat's needs, so they needed to learn how to do some of these tasks. It is not reassuring when you finally move someone into a nursing home because you can't physically care for them any more, only to learn that you, a "lay person" medically speaking, know more about how to do certain tasks than the professionals do.

Slowly but surely all of us made the necessary adjustments. After the initial dismay that Pat could no longer live most of the time at home, we got used to her being in the nursing home. She was still able to talk, and still occasionally ate a few things by mouth, and it was possible every now and then to take her home for an afternoon.

But all of that changed before too long, and it was no longer either safe or easy to take her out of the nursing home for even a short amount of time. Before long Pat was not able to talk. In fact it has been more than six years since she has been able to speak a word. Thankfully, she is still able to understand what I say to her, if I speak slowly and don't talk about things that are very complicated.

As these realities set in, I found myself becoming increasingly depressed. Not only could we no longer live together, but the person I adore so much was gradually slipping away. It was very difficult not to imagine what the next stages of her decline would be like. Many times I mentally plotted out what was likely ahead of us, and doing so only made me sadder.

But much worse than imagining her decline was dealing with each new stage. Every time her condition became worse, it was much harder emotionally to deal with the changes than I'd anticipated. I had imagined what it would be like but it was always worse, and for a while I wondered why. Before too long I saw the reason. If you imagine what will happen next, you can make yourself feel very sad while you think about that. But the sadness doesn't last, because you know that she has not really reached that new level yet. When she does reach that level, you know that this is real and it won't go away. Seeing how bad things are and knowing that it will only get worse, you cannot help but feel more depressed. Indeed, the reality of what this disease is doing is always worse than whatever I can imagine.

In spite of all of the things that have happened to Pat and continue to happen, she has never complained to anyone about any of it. Of course, being unable to speak, I can't know exactly what she is thinking now. But even before Pat moved into a nursing home, I once asked her what she thought about during the course of a day. She thought for a few minutes and then replied that she didn't really know. I didn't say anything, but I thought to myself that this is probably just as well, because it likely means that she is not thinking about what is happening to her and how depleted her abilities are.

Once Pat was in the nursing home, I soon realized that my only contact with her would be there. I had to be there to see that she received the care she needed, but it quickly became clear that in the nursing home was the only way we could be together at all. Though I still had to manage her care as one would a patient's needs, this is not just *any* patient! This is my wife! When we first met and later decided to marry, there was no way we could have foreseen that our marriage would come to this—relatively short visits together each day in a nursing home. But that's how things have turned out, and rather than spending each day grieving about what is happening so that I can barely function, I am determined not to miss the chance to be with her. Some people comment that this is what keeping marriage vows means. I don't think about that; my only concern is to be sure that whatever she needs is done. And while I'm visiting her, my goal is to do whatever I can to make the day more enjoyable for her. Does she even remember once I leave that I was there? I have no way of knowing. But it is clear that when I am with her, she knows I am there, and I can see to it that things are done to care for her and make her day less boring.

What the Future Might Hold

As I conclude this chapter, I note that all of our sons are now in their thirties, and none has shown any sign of the disease yet. I still fear that none of them may escape, but I keep thinking about the Ecclesiastes passage. God has constructed our lives so that we cannot know what will happen later in life. Our only option is to trust him and get as much done as possible while there is time. Others who don't have and can't get Huntington's aren't guaranteed a long life just because they can't get this disease. And even some people who will get it in the future may also live to see the day when a cure is found. It is best not to give up on life prematurely; even an apparently hopeless situation may turn out much better than anyone could imagine. Use God's grace to accomplish whatever he calls you to do today. Our tomorrows are unknown, and that is just as well, for we don't need to see in advance how our lives will play out. You can't change whatever God has decided about your future, but you can lose today's opportunities by worrying about tomorrows that may never happen and that can't be changed if they do. This is not a matter of going irresponsibly and blindly into the future. It is a matter of handling well the time God has given us (our todays), and about leaving our tomorrows in God's hands. When we get to tomorrow, it may be different than we expect or will like. But one thing will be the same: The God who is in charge today and who gives comfort, strength, and grace to handle today's challenges will be there tomorrow to do exactly the same for those who ask him!

PROVIDENCE AND THE PURPOSE OF OUR LIVES

In looking at things that have happened in my life, some might say there is little evidence of God's control or concern, and that my life has been driven one way or another by random events that have no relation to one another. I fully understand that evaluation, and I can affirm that though some things in my life have been like I had anticipated, the exact course of my life has been significantly different than I expected. Even so, as I think about what has happened, I can quite clearly see God's hand in my life, even in the things I never imagined might happen.

For reasons I shared in earlier chapters, I am certain that I would have always been interested in the problem of evil and suffering, even if my family had been completely healthy and had lived a more "normal" life. But I also know that one of the major things God wanted to do with my life was to prepare me for the experience of dealing with tragedy so that I would ultimately think even more deeply about the problem of evil, write about it extensively, and preach and teach on this topic. In addition, all along God knew that Pat would get this disease, and he wanted her to have someone to care for her, and he chose me to be the one. Let me address each of these purposes independently, though to a certain extent they are interrelated.

As for my work and ministry in relation to the problem of evil, so many things in my background point in that direction. I have shared about the concerns raised by my mother's health. Her situation, plus other examples of godly people I knew who suffered stimulated in me an interest in the problem of evil. Because of that interest, my education at several schools made that issue a focus of my thinking and work for degree programs in which I enrolled.

All of that work and thought, however, might have stayed with me alone if not for God's call to ministry. Relatively early in my life, I sensed the Lord's call to preach and teach, a call to full-time ministry. By the time I entered high school, I was convinced the Lord wanted me to train others for ministry—a teaching ministry similar to my dad's seemed to be God's design for my life. I also believed that God wanted me to preach and serve as a pastor. I wasn't sure how that would fit with full-time teaching, but I figured God had all of that planned and that at the right time he would show me when to teach and when to pastor.

Of course, during the early years of my education I never envisioned the specific subject matter I would pursue in school and as a teacher and writer. Learning languages always came very easy for me, so in high school and college I probably thought that I would eventually teach Greek or Hebrew and be an Old Testament or New Testament scholar. But once I entered seminary and enrolled in a degree program designed to train men and women for ministry, I quickly saw that my greatest interest was in dealing with ideas. That meant theology would be the focus of my study and ministry. I had always heard that it is important and helpful for theologians to know philosophy, but I wasn't quite sure why. Eventually, the Lord opened the door for me to study philosophy at the doctoral level at the University of Chicago. Once I started taking courses I realized how much philosophy interested me and I began to understand how and why it is important to systematic theology.

In all of these things, I was sure that I was doing what God wanted me to do. I wasn't exactly clear as to why he wanted me to do doctoral studies in philosophy instead of theology, but as I took philosophy courses I saw how this information would help me to be a better theologian. But even more fundamentally, I could see how my course of studies was dramatically enhancing my ability to think. After finishing my course work and comprehensive exams, it was time to begin a doctoral dissertation. I wanted to work on the problem of evil, but I doubted that at a major secular university I would be allowed to write on a subject handled in traditional philosophy of religion. But there was no hesitation on the part of my dissertation readers. I still marvel at the open-mindedness of my professors and the university in allowing me not only to write on this issue but to defend a theistic position!

Given my background and upbringing, it is easy to see why I was so interested in the problem of evil. You can also see how my earlier degree theses on the book of Job and on God's sovereignty in relation to human freedom both stimulated and prepared me to work on the problem of evil for my dissertation. I completed my doctoral program in 1978, but I began teaching in 1976. The issue of God and evil arose in a number of courses I taught. I could see how so much in my life had led me to the teaching ministry I was having. And, after my graduation in 1978, I just assumed that I would continue teaching and writing on this topic (and others). I thought I had worked out good answers to this problem—and thankfully, my dissertation committee thought so too. Of course, if I was to communicate the content of my studies to everyday people, I knew that I would have to revise my material to make the same points without all the technicalities one would expect in a doctoral dissertation. But I believed I had the basic answers to this problem. When I heard of Christians struggling with various afflictions, I wished that I could share with them insights from my dissertation. I thought that would resolve their doubts and remove their pain.

When we learned in 1987 that Pat had Huntington's, I was totally shocked and surprised. I have already shared in an earlier chapter how all my previous academic work was of no comfort at that time. I couldn't understand what was happening, but looking back, I can easily see God's hand in the ordering of the various events in my life. If we had received the diagnosis before I had done the intellectual work on the problem of evil, I probably would have spent a lot of time searching for solutions to my intellectual questions in philosophical discussions of the problem of evil. In light of the emotional, physical, and spiritual pain I was experiencing after Pat's diagnosis, I doubt that I would have been in a frame of mind that would have allowed me to do the hard philosophical work I undoubtedly would have thought necessary. I probably would have thought that I could apply philosophy to our situation, and yet, if I had tried to do so, that would have only led to more frustration. I likely would have despaired of ever making any sense of what was happening. As things actually did happen, I remember that for months after getting Pat's diagnosis, I was distraught by the thought that I was teaching students theology (the study of God's being, his acts, and his relationships) and yet with what had happened, I wasn't sure I knew anything about God. I shudder to think of what I might have thought and done at that time if I hadn't previously done all the academic study about the problem of evil.

By leading me through the academic journey I had experienced *before* I had to deal with real suffering in a personal way, God in effect was preparing me to look elsewhere than my academic studies for answers to what was happening in my life and why. From your reading of the things I've shared in this book, you have seen, I trust, that what I needed to learn is not to be found in any theology or philosophy text. But without my studies in theology and philosophy, I probably would have searched for answers in the study of theology and philosophy to what we were experiencing. Hopefully, I would have eventually come to see that the personal problem of dealing with suffering is not handled by theology and philosophy alone, but who knows? I can clearly see the Lord's hand in the very timing of the events in my life, including his providential guidance in what I studied and when I studied it!

I can also see God's hand in what I have done with all my thinking about the religious problem of evil—the problem about one's personal struggle with pain and suffering and how that affects one's relationship with God. Shortly after receiving my PhD, I was able to get my dissertation published, but it didn't stay in print very long. After it went out of print, I approached another publisher, and received a contract to revise the book a bit and reprint it. I believe this contract came before we found out about Pat's condition. Once we did learn about her Huntington's, everything in my life was put on hold, including my work on publications. When I eventually returned to my work on the problem of evil, I found that the academic discussion had changed significantly in the years since I finished my dissertation. Hence, many new chapters were written for that reprint. As I worked on those chapters, I began to think that maybe the best way to make my point that the religious problem of evil is a different kind of problem from the others would be to write about my wife and family. I concluded that if I did this, I would have to adopt a much more direct, nontechnical style, and I had to share explicitly my thoughts and feelings about what was happening; otherwise the material probably wouldn't help anyone, especially suffering people, very much.

Somewhat reluctantly, I wrote two relatively brief chapters that were included in my longer work on the academic problem of evil. The manuscript was delivered to the publisher in 1993, and I thought that would be the end of what I would do on this topic. But God had other plans. When editors at the press read the two chapters on the religious problem of evil, they immediately encouraged me to take that material out of the original book, expand it, and publish it as a more popular-level book. I appreciated their endorsement of the work, but I was hesitant to do what they suggested. However, as I thought further about their suggestion and began to speak to classes about Pat's condition and what the Lord was teaching me through it, I received many positive reactions to this material. In addition, people who read the longer work often commented on the helpfulness of the two chapters on the religious problem of evil. After some thought and prayer, I concluded that even though I wasn't eager to write this further book, if the Lord wanted to use it to help others, I shouldn't stand in his way. The result eventually was a popular-level book on the religious problem of evil, a work that comprises much of the content of this current book.

It is quite clear to me, then, that one of the things God wanted to do with my life is bring me through the experiences I've had with evil and suffering so that I would write, teach, and preach on these themes. And his ultimate intention is that what I would say and do would help hurting people deal with tragedy and would also help those who minister to the afflicted. Though I thought God wanted me to write and teach about the problem of evil even before we received Pat's diagnosis, I envisioned presenting very different content than what you have read in this book. Without dealing with Pat's disease and its implications, I could not have written this more popular-level book. Moreover, I certainly couldn't present from the pulpit the more technical academic ideas from my dissertation, but when I share what is happening to my family and talk about my struggles with it, many who hear or read find what I say to be very helpful. I am confident that this was an important part of God's plan all along; these things haven't happened by mere chance.

I also see God's hand in another factor that has contributed to my work on the various problems of evil. In an earlier chapter, I wrote about God hiding information so that I wouldn't hesitate over health issues to marry Pat. There is another respect in which God has hidden the future from all of us, and I think it has contributed to the work I've done on the religious problem of evil. Currently, there is no known cure for Huntington's disease, despite the fact that research on this disease continues. Of course, there is a cure for this disease and God knows what it is, but so far he hasn't divulged it to anyone who has the disease or is at risk, nor has he revealed it to researchers working on this disease. I can't predict when that information will be revealed; everyone who knows about this disease hopes it will be sooner rather than later.

Suppose that a cure had been available even before Pat was diagnosed, or that it was revealed shortly after we learned the dreadful news. Huntington's would still be a horrible disease, but there would be far less mental, emotional, and spiritual turmoil over having the disease if a cure were known. I think it is safe to say that without the stress of dealing with an incurable, terminal disease, I would not have questioned so thoroughly why and how this could be happening, and I wouldn't have discovered many of the things shared in this book.

Please do not misunderstand this. I am not suggesting that God has withheld information about a cure for this disease just so that I would have time to think through these issues and write this book. I don't know why God hasn't allowed researchers to discover a cure yet. But I do know that the delay has been instrumental in accomplishing God's intentions for my specific life history during the years since 1987 when we first learned about this disease. My own thought about and work on the various problems of evil have been spurred in part by the fact that no cure is currently known. God has used this in my life to accomplish some things he wanted to do in and through me.

I also believe that God had another major intention for me, and it relates to marrying Pat. God decided to provide someone to manage Pat's needs and take care of her, and I am that someone. Pat and I might never have met, let alone married. In fact, she might not have married anyone. Even so, God knew she would get this disease and would need someone to take care of her, especially as she became less able to care for herself. That she would get this disease was determined the moment she was conceived.

Over the last two decades or so as I have helplessly watched Pat's condition worsen, I have thought on a number of occasions that the point of this marriage is not about me but about her. For a long time it has been clear that there just isn't any other immediate or extended family member who would be Pat's caregiver. God knew she would need someone, and he does not leave those who faithfully follow him without help in time of need. And so, he provided me.

What I am suggesting may sound contrary to much Christian thinking about the purpose of marriage. Early in life Christians are taught that marriage is God's idea, and that in instituting marriage, he intended to provide a helpmate for man. God said that it is not good for man to be alone. To satisfy the need for a companion and partner, God created woman. It is natural, then, for men to think of marriage in terms of finding a wife who will help them with their life's work. In my case, I knew I needed a wife to help with my ministry. When I met Pat, I had no problems with her having a call to full-time ministry, for I believed she could and would basically fulfill that call as my wife. That wouldn't mean she couldn't also minister apart from my ministry, but helping me would be a major part of her life. So I adopted the common Christian understanding of marriage.

I must affirm as strongly as possible that Pat has been a wonderful wife and supporter and helper of my ministry. But in light of her condition, I believe that God's purpose in bringing us together was as much (if not more so) to provide someone to care for her as it was to give me a helper for my ministry. And I want to say as clearly as I can that if this is the major purpose of my marrying Pat, I have no problem with that! It is a privilege to be her husband, and I am more than willing to do whatever is needed to care for her. If the tables were turned, I have no doubt that she would eagerly care for me.

Some may read this and respond that while this has happened to us, we can hardly say that God's intention (even his main intention) with our marriage was to provide someone to care for Pat. It's just something that turned out that way, but not evidence of God's providence at work. I disagree, and I want to explain why.

Looked at from one perspective, I suppose it might appear that all of this has happened somewhat by chance. Indeed, when you think about it, it seems that it was a long shot that Pat and I would ever even meet, let alone marry and raise a family. Pat was raised in upstate New York in North Syracuse. Wheaton, Illinois, was the farthest west Pat had ever been, and that hadn't happened until she entered a master's program at Wheaton College in 1971.

As for me, I'm three years older than Pat. I was born in Dallas, Texas, but raised in Southern California from the time I was two years old. I had heard of Syracuse, New York, but the basic thing I knew about it was that Syracuse University, located in that city, usually had a pretty good football team. I had been to Chicago a few times to visit my brother who went there in 1966 to take a teaching position at Moody Bible Institute, but most of my life I had lived in Southern California. When I did move to the Chicago area in 1971, it was to attend Trinity Evangelical Divinity School, not Wheaton College. Trinity and Wheaton are geographically about thirty-five miles apart. That doesn't sound like a long distance, but those familiar with metropolitan Chicago and its traffic know that these two schools are located in suburbs that seem worlds apart.

In the summer of 1971 I moved to the Chicago area in preparation for my studies at Trinity. From July 1971 to the start of February 1972 I dated many girls, most of whom I'd met through my connections with Trinity. It wasn't until late February of 1972 that I met Pat, and even then, that happened on a blind date.

With such diverse backgrounds, what are the *chances* that Pat and I would ever even meet? Quite small, but that just underscores my point: none of this has happened by chance! One can choose to say that all of this was totally a happy series of coincidences coming together by chance. However, with everything I have shared about our story, I trust that you can see why it makes much more sense to see God's providential hand at work in our lives to bring these things to pass. Though I wish Pat didn't have this disease, because I can see so clearly that God's hand has brought all of these things to pass, I find it easier to accept the roles God intended me to fulfill. If I thought (or even suspected) that what has happened was not under God's providential control, the burdens I have to bear would be absolutely intolerable!

Having said these things about divine providence, there is one further point I must make about God's will. In seeking God's will it is important to distinguish between God's will and his way, and there is also God's timing. My point is that at times we feel led by the Lord to do something, but we also mentally construct the way it will happen and when it will occur. In contrast, God may plan it to happen in a different way and with different timing. As events start to play out and events don't go exactly as we thought, it is very natural to question whether we have misread God's will altogether. In the aftermath of receiving Pat's diagnosis in November 1987, I know that I raised just that question. I had figured out what I thought God wanted me to do and I had constructed my plan for how it would happen. When I learned that things weren't going to happen as I had thought, it was natural to wonder whether the path taken really was God's will.

In spite of those doubts, I know that God wanted Pat and me

to marry, that he had called both of us to full-time ministry, and that he wanted us to have children. I just expected all of this to happen in a different way than it did, a way that I had constructed as a best-case scenario. What I had to do was readjust my thinking to the reality that even if we know what God wants us to do (his will), that doesn't automatically dictate the way his will comes to pass. And it certainly doesn't mean that we can do whatever we want whenever and however we choose so long as the result is what we sensed is God's will for us. God's will must be done in his way and in his timing. Readjusting my thinking to God's way and timing has been painful but necessary. But I can now see that the way events have happened is the way God intended to accomplish his will in our lives. Could he have done it in some other way? Only he knows the answer to that. But he certainly knew that the way things have happened would move Pat and me to do his will. It is natural to suspect that there must have been a less painful way to get us to do what he wanted. But because I believe that God knows things none of us knows and is both all-loving and all-wise, I must simply accept the path he chose for us as the proper way to accomplish his will most fully in our lives. I cannot prove rationally (or otherwise) beyond a shadow of a doubt that what I've just written is correct; that's where faith comes in. I think sometimes God brings very difficult and confusing things into our lives, things that we can't entirely figure out rationally, so that we get a chance to exercise the faith we say is at the heart of our relationship to God. Is it wrong for God to do that? I don't see how it could be!

As for God's specific path for our lives, the Lord did want me to marry Pat and to have a ministry of teaching, preaching, and writing. It's just that all of this has happened under different circumstances than we had envisioned and with a slightly different emphasis than I had in mind. In addition, God wanted not only Pat but me as well to serve him on the mission field. Beginning in 1985, Pat and I traveled together and ministered on many occasions, literally all over the world. We originally thought of missions in terms of long-term missions, but God's way was for us to go as short-term missionaries during my summer breaks to teach those training for ministry and to preach in a variety of settings. In fact, in summer 2001 we even made it to Africa, ministering both in South Africa and Zimbabwe.

There is God's will and there is God's way, and all of this must be within his timing. I have learned that everyone needs to think outside the box of our notions about how God will accomplish his will in our life. It is, of course, possible that anyone may misjudge both God's way and his will, but even so, we must be open to the possibility that while we are reading God's goal for us correctly, we must be flexible enough to let him accomplish it in his own way and timing.

As I conclude this chapter and book, I hope that what I have written has ministered to you, and that it will help you serve others who are hurting. This has not been an easy book to write, and I suspect that some things I've written are hard for you to read. I wish I had learned in a different way the principles these experiences have taught me, but I didn't, and I have shared what has happened and what I have learned from it in hope that what I've written will help you.

As for me and my family, the story continues. Just as there have been surprises already (some welcome, some unwelcome), God probably has others in store. Do I have any regrets over marrying Pat and having a family? If this question means would I have married her if I knew then what I know now, the question is really impossible to answer. If I knew then what I know now, I would have known what a blessing from God she and my sons would be. I would have known all the problems I'd avoid by not marrying her, but I'd also have known of the lost blessings. Would I give back those incredible blessings to escape the trials we have experienced? While many of us might wish for a different life, that is probably because we think a different life would be one with no problems, or at least one with nothing catastrophic. But in a fallen world there can be no guarantees of a life with only happiness and no problems or challenges. So perhaps I could have avoided the pains and sorrows that have come our way. But a different life might have had different but even worse problems than those we have experienced. I certainly know that I have received many great blessings, and I wouldn't want to lose them!

Some things are certain for me. I know that throughout eternity I'll be thanking God for the wife and family he gave me and for the ministry he has allowed us to have in spite of (and even because of) the hardships we have faced and will yet face. I also know that when the wounds from the spiritual warfare in which we all are engaged come—and they will come—we will need the comfort, care, and presence of God. When we first received the news about Pat's disease, I couldn't see how I could both deal with Pat's disease and have the ministry to which I thought God had called me. But more than twenty-eight years after getting her diagnosis, I can attest that God has enabled me to do both. In May of 2015, I completed my thirty-ninth *consecutive* year of teaching. In all that time, I have never completely missed a ministry assignment because of a need related to Pat's disease that had to be handled immediately. In fact, I can only remember one class session that ended early because I had to care for her.

Remarkable, you are probably thinking. Indeed it is! God doesn't give us a task that we can't do. Even more, when he gives a task, he is present to help us do what he asks. As we have lived with Pat's disease, I have been faced with the increasing presence of her absence. Oh, she is still alive, but she is increasingly trapped in a body. It has been and is painful to watch and to be able to do nothing to help her recover. If I focus only on that, there is cause for much despair. But most of the time I do not find myself immobilized by grief and unable to function. I can only explain that by the fact that in everything that is happening I am certain of God's presence and sustaining grace. Can I prove that God is there? Probably not in the sense of proof a philosopher would require. But even so, there are just some things that faith knows!

As you deal with trials and suffering, may you find the comfort and sustaining grace that only God can give!

AFTERWORD

By Patricia S. Feinberg

I would like to tell you what God has done in my life. As my brother and I were growing up, our mother suffered with a mysterious disease. I did not know the name of the disease, nor the specifics of it, because we were not told. My personal opinion was that it was a mental illness, and most of my mother's symptoms suggested that to me. It was only much later that we would learn she had Huntington's disease.

My family was not a Christian family at the outset, but the Lord gave both my mother and me a desire to know him. My mother sold Avon products for a while, and she made a friend on her route who was a Christian. My mother's friend invited her to an evangelism meeting where she accepted Christ. The pastor from the friend's church came over and talked with my father, who also became a Christian. My brother and I came to the Lord when a missionary candidate from the church came to talk with us.

I was nine years old at the time. As God gave me a desire to follow him, I started reading my Bible every day and attending the church. Over the years I became very involved in the church.

The youth pastor in my church had been a missionary to Africa, and he was a great influence on me. When he preached at a missionary conference where an invitation was given for young people to follow the Lord completely in their lives, I turned my life over to God for whatever he wanted me to do. I thought he might want me on the mission field, so I took steps to prepare myself for that. I went to Nyack College, in part because it had a strong reputation for training missionaries. After graduation I applied to some mission boards, but nothing opened up. Therefore I went on to Wheaton College for a master's degree in Christian Education. I felt such additional training would help me in mission work, and I thought that after further academic work, the Lord would open up the opportunity for me to go to the mission field.

While at Wheaton, our prayer group prayed that if the Lord had a husband for us, he would bring him along at the right time. One of my friends in the group was dating a student at Trinity Seminary, and she arranged a blind date for me with another seminarian attending Trinity.

As it turned out, John and I dated not just once but many times. As our relationship grew, the Lord made it clear that he wanted us to marry. We felt certain that God had led us together. After several years of marriage, we were blessed with three special boys who have been a continual joy to us.

In the midst of raising a family and sharing in John's ministry, I learned in the fall of 1987 that I have a genetic neurological disease called Huntington's chorea. It involves the premature deterioration of the brain, and it can have severe mental and physical effects. In addition, it shortens one's life. Though I was extremely shocked when this disease was diagnosed, I knew that when physical problems come, one should thank God for his presence and strength in the midst of those problems, rather than becoming bitter. And I knew that I should do that whether or not I felt like it; so that's what I did on the way home in the car. I also knew 1 Thessalonians 5:18 which says, "Give thanks in all circumstances, for this is God's will for you in Christ Jesus." No matter what the circumstances, God is still there, and he is in control of all that happens. He is faithful to his Word. That is reason for thanksgiving, and I continue to thank him each day.

The next months were very difficult for both John and me, going through the process of accepting what had happened. One thing that was very helpful to me was that as I read through the book of Psalms, I wrote down every reference having to do with God's strength in time of trouble. The main one was Psalm 46:1, "God is our refuge and strength, an ever-present help in trouble." God made that verse true in my life. I have confidence in his presence, even in the midst of this disease.

I have been trying to figure out what God wants me to learn from this, and what he wants me to do about it. One thing the Lord has reinforced to me is that I am just clay in his hands. As Paul says in Romans 9:20, "But who are you, O man, to talk back to God? Shall what is formed say to him who formed it, 'Why did you make me like this?'" God has the right to do anything he wants with me. Who am I to complain?

I gave myself to Christ as a teenager for whatever he wanted—without reservation. Though what has happened is not at all what I imagined, I cannot complain. I said he could do with me as he chose. Far from complaining, it is my responsibility to thank God for doing his will in my life.

Another thing God has done through this illness is to make me face life and death issues and to see the absolute necessity of making the most of the time I have left. It is easy for all of us to think there will be enough time to do what needs to be done for the Lord. We tend to plan to serve him, but always later. My experience is a vivid reminder that no one of us has a guarantee of how long our life on earth will be or what kind of life we will have. Whatever God calls us to do in service of the kingdom needs to be done sooner, not later.

Another Scripture that God has used in my life is 2 Corinthians

1:3–4: "Praise be to the God and Father of our Lord Jesus Christ, the Father of compassion and the God of all comfort, who comforts us in all our troubles, so that we can comfort those in any trouble with the comfort we ourselves have received from God." The Lord has given me such complete comfort that I want to find ways to share it with others.

My disease has also offered witnessing opportunities. One opportunity that John and I had was the chance to witness to my Jewish neurologist. John went with me to see her, and she came right out and asked us what he was doing teaching in a Christian seminary when he has a Jewish last name. In telling her how his family came out of Judaism to Christ, he was able to share the gospel with her. The other thing that she could not understand was how calm we were about the whole thing.

I consider it another blessing of the Lord that the disease for many years progressed extremely slowly. That has amazed the doctors from the beginning, and it gives us a further opportunity to witness to them. When they express their amazement, we make a point to share our belief that my disease and my very life are in God's hands. I believe the course the disease has taken is a result of God's intervention on my behalf.

It has been many years since we learned that I have Huntington's. God has been so faithful to me, and I thank him for his faithfulness, love, and comfort. It is my hope that what I have shared will be a comfort and encouragement to you, the readers. I want to say to those who are suffering that God is sufficient!

1996

APPENDIX

The Uses of Affliction

Though God isn't the author of evil and suffering, he does allow these things to happen. When they do, he is not helpless to use them to accomplish positive things in our lives. While the affliction isn't good, it can serve as an occasion for God to bring some good out of what is evil. The facts that God does this and that we can see him working in our lives can reassure us that his hand is still upon us. He isn't angry at us, and we aren't abandoned. Realizing that God didn't bring this affliction but is doing something positive in the midst of it can help us realize that the Creator is good and that he is worthy of our worship.

I am addressing this topic because some people feel that afflictions are not only painful, but they also serve no positive use in our lives. Hence, there seems to be no good reason for God to allow us to experience them. In the text of this book I have shared some of the reasons God allows his people to undergo affliction. Though you may feel that at least some of those reasons justify God letting us experience these trials, you may wonder whether there is or even can be any other positive thing that might come from the trials and afflictions we suffer.

In response I want to present a series of things God can do in the life of the afflicted. I have found this material on the ways God can use suffering in our lives encouraging, though it wasn't particularly helpful in the earlier stages of my own struggles. When someone is still reeling from the shock of tragedy, it won't likely help to say, "Take heart, there are many positive things God can do through this affliction, and I want to share them with you." At that point, the sufferer is too hurt, too angry, and too much in shock to grasp fully the import of this information. If you begin to rehearse the beneficial uses of suffering, the sufferer may quickly inform you that he or she would gladly forgo any of these positive things since they require us to experience affliction in order to get them. Or the sufferer may simply ask why, if God can bring good out of evil, he can't bring good out of good.

If you get these (or other) negative responses, it is wisest to see that the sufferer needs some time to begin healing before he or she will be in a frame of mind to entertain the idea that something good might come from something so painful and evil. Hopefully, at some later point in the healing process, the sufferer will be ready to hear the things that follow.

Before I present possible uses of suffering, I must be clear about what the following information does not mean. Pointing to the uses of suffering may seem to mean that these positive outcomes are the reasons God allows suffering in the first place. It may even appear that I am saying these uses of suffering prove that God is a good God in spite of the evil in our world.

Neither of these ideas is my point, for I don't believe either to be correct. If I were espousing such views, I would be saying that God is a good God despite the fact that he hasn't removed suffering and evil because he is able to use evil as a means to accomplish a good end. But to say that is to say that the end justifies the means. I don't hold that view of right and wrong, and I don't believe Scripture teaches such an ethic.

The information I'll share is not meant to *justify* God's ways to mankind, the sort of thing Christian philosophers and theologians do when they tackle intellectual questions about why an all-loving, all-powerful God would allow evil in our world. I have addressed such questions elsewhere at length.*

There is a difference, however, between justifying God as good in spite of evil and helping the afflicted feel more positive toward God in spite of their affliction. Many things can help remove emotional and spiritual pain as the afflicted seek to live at peace with the God who has allowed this pain. What I offer now is help for healing the breach in the sufferer's relationship with God. Of course, no one can guarantee whether and when in the process of suffering the things I'll share will help. But they might help, and whether or not they do, the things I'll present come from biblical teaching about suffering and the believer.

How, then, might God use affliction positively in the life of the righteous sufferer?** There are many ways, and I have divided them into *ten basic categories.* It is natural to think that in any given instance of suffering, God is using it to accomplish only one thing. If we don't immediately sense what that is, frustration can arise. However, in any actual case God may intend to accomplish a whole series of things rather than just one, and not just in the life of the sufferer alone. God may intend to accomplish something in the sufferer's life, something in the lives of those who know the sufferer, and something in regard to angelic and demonic forces.

---

*See my *The Many Faces of Evil: Theological Systems and the Problems of Evil*, rev. and exp. ed. (Wheaton, IL: Crossway, 2004).

**The questions of why the unrighteous suffer and how God uses affliction in their lives are also important. However, the more troublesome religious problems focus on righteous suffering. While God may use affliction in the life of unbelievers to accomplish some of the same goals he intends for believers, he might also use affliction of the unbelieving as punishment for their sin. It should also be clear that in speaking of righteous sufferers, I am not referring to people who are sinlessly perfect. Only Christ fits that description. Rather, I refer to those believers whose basic pattern of life is to follow God and avoid evil.

A particular case of suffering may have several goals God wants to accomplish.

First, God may allow affliction for the same reason he did in the case recorded in John 9:1–3. In that situation and now, *affliction provides an opportunity for God to manifest his power.* In John 9, the disciples asked Jesus about a man who was blind from birth: "Who sinned, this man or his parents, that he was born blind?" Jesus rejected the common belief that all suffering must be a punishment for some specific sin. "'Neither this man nor his parents sinned,' said Jesus, 'but this happened so that the work of God might be displayed in his life.'" To the amazement of those who saw it, Christ then performed a miracle to restore the man's sight. Similarly, God sometimes allows affliction in the life of the righteous as a basis for some future work that demonstrates his power and glory.

During earlier years of Pat's dealing with Huntington's, we saw this happen to some extent. Though she showed some signs of the disease, doctors repeatedly mentioned how wonderful it was that the disease had progressed so slowly for so long. On more than one occasion we used those comments as an opportunity to state our belief that we weren't just lucky. Rather, this was evidence of the hand of God in her life. Even though her condition is now significantly worse, that doesn't negate the display of God's power in Pat's case in the early stages of this disease.

Second, *God may use affliction to remove a cause for boasting.* When things go smoothly in life, we tend to feel self-sufficient. Affliction reminds us that we aren't, and that we must ultimately rely on God. A classic illustration of this principle comes from the life of the apostle Paul. Paul had a thorn in the flesh, some sort of physical ailment whose exact nature Bible scholars debate. In 2 Corinthians 12:8–9, Paul says he pleaded with God to remove the thorn, but God didn't. Paul wrote that if God had removed the problem, he might have thought too highly of himself in view of the significant revelations God had given to him (v. 7). His thorn in the flesh was a constant reminder that even though God had revealed many important things to him (things that Paul ultimately wrote about which wound up as Scripture), he shouldn't assume that meant that he was a super-Christian, someone God was lucky to have on his team! Sometimes God uses affliction similarly in our lives.

In the first two chapters of Job, we see a third way God uses the suffering of the righteous. *God allows afflictions at least in part to show Satan genuine faith.* Satan claimed that the only reason Job served God was that it paid Job to do so. Look at all the blessings God had given him! Satan slanderously predicted that if God removed his blessings from Job, Job would no longer serve him. God answered that Job served him out of genuine love, and he decided to prove that to Satan. Through Job's afflictions and through his unswerving faithfulness to God, Satan saw that there are those who actually do serve God out of true love, not just because it pays to do so.

God may use affliction in our life to accomplish some purpose *for us,* and at the same time use our response to show Satan and his legions that even today there are still people who love and serve God regardless of their personal circumstances in life. Others will see this as well. This is extremely important, for as Christians we claim to have the ultimate answers to life's problems. Of course, it is relatively easy to make such claims and to be a Christian when everything is going well. What many non-Christians want to know, however, is whether Christianity works when things go wrong. That's one of the true tests of any religion. If we turn from God in the midst of affliction, we communicate to those watching that at times of stress Christianity offers no more of an answer than any other religion or ideology. God still needs people today who will show others that when life brings the unexpected and even the tragic, they will continue to love and serve God, not because it pays to do so, but because he is worthy of devotion.

This is why Peter tells us that in the midst of affliction we must be ready to explain why we continue to hold on to our hope in God (1 Peter 3:15). This verse is frequently taken out of context to show that Christians should always defend the faith in general. That is, the academic discipline of apologetics should be encouraged. However, that is neither the point nor the context of this verse. In 1 Peter 3, Peter addresses suffering for the sake of righteousness as a follower of Christ. Many of Peter's readers were experiencing persecution for their faith. No doubt there were people who laughed at these Christians' faith, claiming that it could not protect them from the persecution they were experiencing. Peter instructed these Christians (and all of us) that when affliction comes, and we are challenged to explain why we continue to trust God and remain faithful to him in spite of what has happened, we must be ready to defend our continued hope. Our hope is that there is a God who knows what we are experiencing and cares. It is a hope that God will right the wrong that others do to afflict us. And it is a hope that God will deliver us from the pain and suffering we are enduring and that he will grant us his sustaining grace until he does remove the trial! Peter added that our response must be both verbal and nonverbal (1 Peter 3:15–17). That is, we must not only explain why we have hope and why Christianity makes a difference, but we must live as people for whom Christianity makes a real difference. We dare not use our affliction as an excuse to justify deserting Christian principles and disobeying God's Word.

Fourth, sometimes *God uses affliction as an opportunity to demonstrate to believers and nonbelievers the concept of the body of Christ.* According to 1 Corinthians 12:12–26, each believer in Christ as Savior is a member of the body of Christ. We are related to one another through Christ, and we need each other. Verse 26 says, "If one part suffers, every part suffers with it." That means that when one suffers, all suffer, and when one rejoices, everyone rejoices. This is the ideal, but it doesn't always match our experience. Too often Christians treat one another as if there were total isolation among members of the body of Christ. To correct this mistaken attitude, God may on occasion use the affliction of one member of the body to show other members that believers need each other and must help one another.

Through affliction the body of Christ concept may be demonstrated in several different ways. Suffering gives opportunity for afflicted people to experience the compassionate love of God through other believers. It allows sufferers to understand experientially what it means to have their burdens carried (Gal. 6:2). These truths have been vividly displayed to us on many occasions through the words and deeds of believers who care.

In addition, suffering gives other believers the opportunity to express Christian love to those in need. When we help afflicted members of the body, we understand more fully how deeply we need one another. We experience as well what it means to show Christian love and compassion. In order to give us that opportunity to minister, God may allow affliction to strike another member of our spiritual family.

Jesus said that people would know that believers are his disciples if we love one another. Helping a suffering brother or sister is a tangible way to show that we are followers of Christ.

Fifth, Scripture also teaches that *in a number of ways affliction in the life of the righteous can and does promote holiness.* First Peter 4:1–2 makes the general point that the experience of suffering helps the believer to put away sin. Peter writes:

Therefore, since Christ suffered in his body, arm yourselves also with the same attitude, because he who has suffered in his body is done with sin. As a result, he does not live the rest of his earthly life for evil human desires, but rather for the will of God.

When Peter says the sufferer "is done with sin," he does not mean that by suffering the believer is completely removed from the power, influence, or guilt of sin. As 1 John 1:8 teaches, "If we claim to be without sin, we deceive ourselves and the truth is not in us." It is impossible to remove sin's influence completely in this life. Instead, Peter means that afflictions have a way of driving believers away from committing specific acts of sin. They do so by helping us resist the temptations that surround us rather than yielding to them. When affliction keeps us from committing specific acts of sin, we draw closer to the Lord, and view things more with the significance that he puts on them. This is evidence of the Holy Spirit at work in us to help us grow in holiness and conformity to the character of Jesus Christ.

Affliction promotes holiness, or sanctification, by refining our faith. First Peter 1:6–7 says,

> In this you greatly rejoice, though now for a little while you may have had to suffer grief in all kinds of trials. These have come so that your faith—of greater worth than gold, which perishes even though refined by fire—may be proved genuine and may result in praise, glory and honor when Jesus Christ is revealed.

The focus of this test of faith isn't the test itself, but the outcome of the test. That is, the focus is the residue of faith that remains when the test is over. Peter's point isn't that the test itself is precious, for the test is suffering, and that is not more precious than gold. Rather, the faith left after the test is precious. Therefore, as Peter says, believers can endure afflictions because through these experiences God is refining their faith. The ultimate result is that at Christ's appearing the believer's tested faith will be found genuine and will result in praise and honor and glory to God.

Holiness is also promoted by suffering, when God uses it to edu-cate believers in ways that cause them to grow closer to the Lord and to be more Christlike. For example, James 1:3–4, Romans 5:3–4, and 1 Peter 5:10 teach that God develops in us perseverance or endurance through adversity. Hebrews 5:8 states that even Christ in his humanity learned obedience through suffering. Now, if God is to teach us anything, he must have our attention. When there is no affliction in our lives, it is easy to become overly self-sufficient and inattentive to what the Lord wants to teach us as he desires to draw us closer to himself. When affliction comes, though we may be inclined to rebel against God, if we pay attention to what God is trying to teach us, we may instead learn things we might not otherwise have been open to hear.

Through difficult experiences believers can also draw closer to the Lord by catching a glimpse of his sovereignty and majesty such as they have never seen before. Job 42:2–4 records the response of a man who suffered as much as anyone has ever suffered. Even though Job was righteous (Job 1:8, 21–22; 2:3, 10), he still experienced great trials and pain—and he sought God to understand why. God finally answered Job (chapters 38–41), overwhelming him with a sense of God's power and majesty. As a result, Job exclaimed (42:2–4) that he now understood that God could do anything. In our case as well, sometimes our view of God is far too small, and God expands that view by sending afflictions and proving himself to be the all-powerful One on our behalf. Like Job, we draw closer to the Lord as we come to know him better.

Suffering also produces sanctification because it leads to intimacy with God. Again Job's case is instructive. Even though Job had grown in the Lord before his suffering, he needed to draw closer. At the end of his ordeal, his comments show that he had come to know God more deeply than ever before. He says, "My ears had heard of you but now my eyes have seen you" (Job 42:5). Job's mere hearsay knowledge of God became firsthand experience. There is nothing like affliction to change intellectual abstractions about God's sovereignty, comfort, and concern into concrete realities.

Affliction can stimulate sanctification in yet another way. *God may use affliction to challenge the righteous to growth instead of sin.* This point arises from James 1:1–12. There, the topic is clearly affliction, whereas later in James 1 the topic is temptation to sin.

The typical Greek word for tribulation, affliction, or suffering is *thlipsis. Thlipsis* never appears in the New Testament in a context where it means temptation. On the other hand, the noun *peirasmos* and the verb *peirazō* are the usual words for temptation and to tempt. In several verses, they indicate a trial or testing (1 Peter 4:12; Acts 9:26; 16:7; 24:6; and Rev. 2:2 are examples). However, those verses don't emphasize affliction or suffering, but rather putting someone to a test. In light of these basic New Testament uses of *thlipsis* and *peirasmos*, we would expect to find *thlipsis* in James 1:1–12 and *peirasmos* in verse 13 and following. Instead, *peirasmos* is used throughout the chapter; *thlipsis* doesn't appear at all. This leads me to ask the following questions: Is James suggesting that afflictions are temptations or trials? Are all temptations afflictions? Are all afflictions temptations?

The answer to the first question is debatable, but the second and third questions are easier to answer. Are all temptations afflictions? Obviously, they are not. Some temptations come in the midst of afflictions (for example, the temptation to curse God that confronted Job as he suffered), but many times temptation arises without any accompanying affliction at all.

Are all afflictions temptations? All afflictions are *potentially* temptations because they provide an occasion for us to be tempted. For example, when someone suffering is angry at God, that person is tempted to turn from him. The sufferer may yield to that temptation, but he may instead respond positively in faith and resist the temptation that came from his troubles. When sufferers do resist, the affliction serves as a basis for them to grow closer to the Lord. Perhaps this is implicitly James's point in using *peirasmos* when the term *thlipsis* would seem to be the more natural choice of words.

A final way adversity promotes holiness is by offering sufferers the opportunity to imitate Christ. Many would love to imitate Christ if that meant having his power, glory, and authority over all things. We are called, however, to imitate Christ in other ways. Those who suffer for righteousness may suffer unjustly and for the sake of others. In so doing, they imitate the Savior's example (1 Peter 3:17–18). Moreover, those who suffer as righteous may be required to bear that affliction and persecution without complaint. In so doing, they again follow the pattern of the Lord's behavior (1 Peter 2:21–23).

Jesus put in perspective the whole matter of what his disciples should expect. He said that "a student is not above his teacher, nor a servant above his master. It is enough for the student to be like his teacher, and the servant like his master" (Matt. 10:24–25). If the disciple is to be like his teacher, and if his teacher is Jesus, the disciple can expect to get from society the same thing Jesus did. The people of his own day nailed our Lord to a cross. Can Christian disciples realistically expect to escape persecution?

The apostle John confirms this point as well. He tells us that the children of God can expect their goals, values, and lifestyle to be misunderstood by those outside of Christ, and for the same reasons that Christ was misunderstood (1 John 3:1). The world did not share or understand the Lord's goals and values. The result was that his enemies put him to death.

The more Christlike we become as children of God, the less we can expect to be understood and accepted by the world about us. And the more we can expect to incur the wrath of Satan and the world. Of course, as we imitate Christ in his sufferings, our sanctification or holiness is promoted.

The apostle Paul affirms this as well in Philippians 3. He relates that he left all of his former accomplishments and way of life to follow Christ. In verses 10–11 he states goals that any Christian should want:

I want to know Christ and the power of his resurrection and the fellowship of sharing in his sufferings, becoming like him in his death, and so, somehow, to attain to the resurrection from the dead.

Most Christians, if not all, would certainly desire the first two things Paul offers as his goals. We would love to know Christ better, and who wouldn't want to see in their own life the kind of power that raised Christ from the dead? As to the fellowship of Christ's sufferings, most of us would be happy to forgo that. However, Paul is right in listing this as one of his goals, because it is hard to comprehend how one could really get to know Christ and what he experienced without also undergoing afflictions for the sake of righteousness. We must remember as well that the power that raised Christ from the dead followed his unjust murder on the cross. At least in that case, the power wasn't divorced from the suffering. And so it may be with us. Often it is only when we are totally overwhelmed by the trial and come to the end of our abilities to deal with it that we can bring ourselves to leave it in God's hands and watch his awesome power deliver us.

All of this means that even in the midst of the worst affliction, God is at work to use suffering to draw us closer to him. That doesn't make the grief and pain any less evil, but it should encourage us to realize that affliction isn't always a sign that God has abandoned us.

In addition to using suffering to further our sanctification, a sixth possibility is that *sometimes God uses suffering to prepare us for future ministry and blessing.* For example, sometimes God permits affliction in the life of a godly person for the ministry that is possible in suffering. There are various ways afflicted believers can minister in spite of and even because of their distress. Those who experience adversity can have a tremendous testimony to those who don't know Christ as their personal Savior. Many non-Christians watch very closely how Christians react when they go

through troubles. When they see the righteous experience affliction and remain faithful to the Lord, they are positively impressed.
As Peter says (1 Peter 3:15–16), their persevering faith and the
positive testimony it gives not only puts to silence the negative
thoughts of evil men, but also serves as a positive witness to those
who don't know God personally through Christ.

Just as remaining faithful to God while suffering provides a testimony to non-Christians, doing so can also minister to Christians
as well. Those who remain true to the Lord during hardship serve
as an encouragement to others to remain faithful in spite of their
own problems. Here Peter's words to suffering believers come to
mind. He encourages them to resist the devil and to take a firm
stand for Christ in spite of the afflictions they are enduring. Peter
writes in relation to our adversary (1 Peter 5:9):

> Resist him, standing firm in the faith, because you know that your
> brothers throughout the world are undergoing the same kind of
> sufferings.

Peter's message is clear. You are not the only person suffering
for Christ at the hands of Satan and his legions. All over the world
there are brothers and sisters in Christ who are besieged with trials just as you are suffering. Take heart; you are not alone in this
battle. Others on the firing line haven't surrendered to the enemy
and turned from Christ. Don't you do that either! In addition, God
can and does use afflictions to prepare us to comfort others who
are also undergoing suffering (2 Cor. 1:3–4).

There is also a sense in which those who remain loyal to God in
the midst of trials are actually ministering not only to others but
to themselves as well. That is, as we cling to God in our suffering,
he uses this to prepare us for even greater ministry. Here I think
of the role affliction played even in the life of Christ to prepare
him for further and greater ministry. In Hebrews 2:10 we read,
"In bringing many sons to glory, it was fitting that God, for whom

and through whom everything exists, should make the author of their salvation perfect through suffering."

The words "make perfect" don't refer to sinless perfection. That would make no sense in this case, for Christ has always been perfect! Instead, the words mean "to be brought to completeness or maturity." In other words, Jesus Christ in his humanity was prepared to be the complete Savior (everything a Savior should be) by enduring various afflictions, even before he went to the cross. If God could use adversity to prepare Christ to be our Savior, surely he can also use suffering to prepare us for greater ministry.

Seventh, *God also uses pain and distress to prepare us for further trials.* Just because one difficult trial hits us, that is no reason to think we have had our quota for a whole lifetime. Since we live in a fallen world, we can expect to face further affliction. In fact, there may be even greater and more severe trials yet to come. Had they come sooner, perhaps they would have destroyed us; but God in his goodness and grace prepares us for each new test. Part of that preparation involves confronting and enduring current pains and sorrows.

Think of Abraham. Suppose that in his *first* encounter with God he was required to offer up his son Isaac (Genesis 22). That likely would have been too much for him. God knew that, so he didn't give Abraham the most difficult trial until he had brought him safely through others. Faith and endurance, like other Christian virtues, can grow and develop. One of the ways God helps those virtues grow is by sustaining us successfully through our present trials. He knows exactly how much we can endure at any given moment. Part of God's program of giving us grace to endure each day is to prepare us to receive and use tomorrow's grace when we face that day's challenges!

Eighth, *God uses suffering in the lives of the righteous to prepare them for judgment of their works.* According to 1 Peter 1:7, affliction helps prepare the believer for the coming of Christ. After Christ returns for his church, all believers will give him an account of what they have done in their lives (2 Cor. 5:10; 1 Cor. 3:10–15). In 1 Peter 1:7, Peter writes that affliction helps prepare sufferers for that judgment so that their faith and actions will result in praise, glory, and honor when Jesus Christ is revealed.

The connection between suffering and reward may be unclear, but it can be explained. As we endure afflictions, we should become more Christlike, leading to lives that are likely to be filled with deeds that please God. At judgment time it will be evident that we have built lives of gold, silver, and precious stones, not ones of wood, hay, and straw (1 Cor. 3:12–15). There will be rewards for lives pleasing to God. So rather than interpreting hardship as a sign of God's displeasure, we should realize that God likely wants to use it to prepare us for the day of judgment when our endurance under fire serves as the basis of reward.

Ninth, *God may use our afflictions as a basis for ultimately exalting us.* Peter repeatedly teaches the theme of suffering and glory (1 Peter 1:6–7, 11, 21; 2:12, 19–21; 3:9, 14–22; 4:1, 4, 12–16, 19; 5:1–6, 9–10). The message is quite clear. Those who would be great in God's economy must first be brought low. Peter writes, "Humble yourselves, therefore, under God's mighty hand, that he may lift you up in due time" (1 Peter 5:6). Affliction certainly can and does humble us, but regardless of how much we are humbled, suffering endured for righteousness' sake is clearly a prelude to exaltation. Christ is the prime example of this truth (1 Peter 2:20–21; Phil. 2:5–11). If we want to reign with Christ, we must follow his example of righteous suffering.

Finally, *God may use afflictions as a means to take us to be with himself.* As life comes to an end, our final affliction will usher us into God's presence. This may not seem like a positive thing, but that may be because we don't fully agree with Philippians 1:21,

"For to me, to live is Christ and to die is gain." Neither the apostle Paul nor I am suggesting that we should wish to die, or that death itself is good. The reason for death—sin—and the event itself are not good. But for the believer, death is the doorway to everlasting blessing in God's presence. Therefore, the death of a Christian is not necessarily a sign of God's displeasure. Affliction leading to death may well just be God's way of promoting someone into his presence.

This completes my presentation of the uses of suffering. In a given instance, one or more of these may explain in part God's reasons for allowing evil to befall his people. Perhaps he is doing none of these things in a particular case. But when someone experiences affliction and is angry that God doesn't stop it, pointing to these uses of evil can help relieve the sufferer's feelings of confusion and anger. Of course, sometimes it is impossible to determine exactly why God allows a specific instance of suffering. God may simply want to remind us that his ways are ultimately beyond our scrutiny. At some point we all need to let God be God, and know a few things we don't!

Sufferers may wrestle with a further question. The uses of suffering show that God is able to bring long-range good out of short-range evil. But isn't an all-powerful God also able to bring long-term good out of short-term good? If he can, why doesn't he? Scripture doesn't answer this question, and I am not sure that we can know the answer for certain until we stand in the Lord's presence. I can, however, make a suggestion about what may in part be God's reason for not using short-range good to bring long-range good in a particular situation. My suggestion is this: God wants to work in our lives to accomplish his good purposes. In many cases, as we have seen, he wants to teach us something. Of course, it is very hard to teach someone anything unless you have his or her attention. Affliction has a way of getting our attention like nothing else. Yes, God could bring long-range good out of short-term good, but when we experience nothing but blessing, we tend to be overly self-confident. We might not pay attention to God. If so, whatever else God wants to teach us through the experience will likely be lost.

Is this always the reason God brings long-term good out of short-term evil rather than out of short-term good? Only he knows for sure. But at least this suggests a possible reason for God's accomplishing his goals by means of suffering.

Often, we ask God to keep us from hardship and affliction. When that doesn't happen, it is easy to become angry and to wonder why God hasn't answered our prayer. On the other hand, if we take seriously the fact that our world is fallen and that we are engaged in a spiritual war, we realize better why God doesn't always end our suffering. Rather than requesting exemption altogether from the battle and the wounds that come with it, consider the wise counsel of Phillips Brooks (1835–1893):

Do not pray for easy lives; pray to be stronger [people]! Do not pray for tasks equal to your powers, pray for powers equal to your tasks. Then the doing of your work shall be no miracle, but you shall be a miracle. Every day you shall wonder at yourself, at the richness of life, which has come to you by the grace of God.